THOMAS A HEINZ

FRANK LLOYD WRIGHT

FIELD GUIDE

VOL 1

UPPER GREAT LAKES: MINNESOTA, WISCONSIN, MICHIGAN

A.D. ACADEMY EDITIONS

First published in Great Britain in 1996 by
ACADEMY EDITIONS
an imprint of
ACADEMY GROUP LTD
42 Leinster Gardens, London W2 3AN
Member of the VCH Publishing Group

ISBN: 1 85490 480 9

Distributed to the trade in the USA by
NATIONAL BOOK NETWORK, INC
4720 Boston Way, Lanham, Maryland 20706

Printed and bound in Singapore

■ This Field Guide to Wright buildings of the upper Great Lakes region (Michigan, Minnesota and Wisconsin) is arranged geographically, beginning in the northwest and ending in the southeast of each state. This organizational principle is extended to each cluster of sites and each cluster of buildings. Also included are three buildings that are not technically within these state boundaries but which are close enough to be considered as part of these areas. They are in northern Illinois and in Ontario, Canada, and are located within the guide alongside others in their general area.

A geographical list of buildings lists all sites and buildings within each state alphabetically by city. Major cities such as Minneapolis and Detroit have their suburbs noted as such.

A complete list of all of Wright's buildings is included and is arranged alphabetically by the last name of the original client or, if it is a commercial structure, by the proper name of the building. When a building has an alternative, popular name this is also included. Buildings featured in this volume are identified by page number. Buildings featured in other volumes in the series are identified by volume.

Maps have been drawn from many sources, although the primary source has been the United States Geological Survey, which issues detailed topographic maps for the entire United States. Most of the non-urban buildings can be seen in outline on these maps.

Star Ratings

The rating system used throughout the book is based on the author's opinion and takes into account several important factors: the extent to which Wright's design philosophy is expressed in the individual building; the current condition of the building; the impact of later additions, remodeling or recladding work; and the ease with which the building can be located and viewed. These factors give an overall rating to the property, and no area is weighted over another.

Opus Numbers

The Director of Archives at The Frank Lloyd Wright Foundation, Bruce Brooks Pfeiffer, has put together a list of all of Wright's buildings and projects. He has assigned a reference number to each, based on the year of the project and the chronology of projects within that year. While a few inaccuracies may appear as more information about each item is discovered, this has proved the best method of identifying individual designs. All drawings and photographs in the Foundation's archives are identified with these numbers plus an added code for each individual drawing or photograph. Ideally, this system would be extended to include each piece of furniture and panel of art glass. It is hoped that the inclusion of these Opus Numbers will help to clarify and identify each building and give it a unique position within the total scope of Wright's work.

The full listing was published in the five-volume index to the Wright correspondence which was edited by Anthony Alofsin for the Getty Museum and issued by Garland Press. Hopefully Mr Pfeiffer will publish an independent, updated list outside of the five-volume set.

GPS Numbers

The Global Positioning System (GPS) has now been accepted as an accurate locational device used in sea and air travel. A series of time-keeping satellites send their time out to a receiver which calculates the difference in times between at least three of these satellites, giving a specific location and elevation. These GPS readings are accurate within a very narrow range. Avis and Oldsmobile are developing an on-board receiver for automobiles which will direct the driver to specific locations. Soon cellular telephones and portable computers will be fitted with these devices. GPS co-ordinates are included in this Field Guide as an aid to identifying locations. Portable, hand-held GPS units are extremely accurate and easy to use.

Note to Readers

The publisher and author wish to reassert to the readers that the majority of these properties are privately owned and that the owners' legal rights should be respected accordingly. The publisher and author will accept no responsibility for any action taken against any readers who contravene this notice.

■ There are buildings designed by Frank Lloyd Wright in thirty-five states. They number over four hundred if one includes bridges, windmills, gates and fountains. The Field Guides divide these buildings into groups of roughly equal area between the following regions: Upper Great Lakes, MetroChicago, West and East. The last two include areas outside continental USA, such as Japan in the West volume and England in the East volume. Like most architects, Wright's early projects were for members of his family and close to home, in Spring Green and Oak Park. However, as his

reputation grew, he was commissioned to design buildings more far afield until his was a national practice. Overall the distribution of Wright's work follows the concentration of the population. Most of the clients were independent thinkers who were willing to put up with some of the difficulties often associated with the construction of Wright designed buildings, such as contractors who were reluctant to tackle unusual work and bankers who were hesitant to embrace progressive ideas. In return, the clients received buildings that would give them pleasure as long as they lived in them.

■ Buildings designed by Frank Lloyd Wright are national treasures and should be valued as such. From even the most modest of his designs there is much to learn. These structures provide great insight, yet as experiments in construction and models for living they have been little discussed. Most of these buildings are well known in their communities but are not listed on any historical register and therefore have no legislation to protect them for future generations.

About 89 per cent of the buildings featured in this Field Guide are homes and are still used as private residences. Please respect the privacy of the owners and show courtesy by not walking on the lawns or through the flowerbeds that they take such care in maintaining. Buildings that cannot be seen from public areas are noted, although readers are advised to avoid these buildings and concentrate instead on those that are open to the public or those which can be seen from public areas. The number of buildings open to the public is growing all the time and there are also special tours throughout the year when normally private interiors are opened-up.

There should be a greater awareness of the full range of Wright's work. It is hoped that by providing the location of every one of his buildings in this Field Guide series, more people will come to appreciate the architectural excellence that exists in their own backyard.

It was not at all difficult to have a Wright-designed house and in retrospect it seems amazing that relatively few people took advantage of the opportunity. Perhaps the reason behind this reluctance lay in the stories about Wright's infamous personality, or in the mistaken belief that he only designed for the rich. In addition, many banks were exceptionally conservative and were unprepared to invest in case something went wrong during construction. However, the vast majority of clients stayed in their houses a long time, the banks were always paid, and in all my research I have never come across a story of a client defaulting on a payment. Some clients were so convinced of the value of a Wright-designed property that they became their own contractors. The determined and open-minded were rewarded and will always be remembered for their part in commissioning excellence in architecture, even if the buildings are now demolished.

Most Wright projects could not be built today in the same way due to restrictive modern building codes which outlaw the trench/ballast foundation, multi-layered plywood walls, and several other innovations. These buildings prove that creative approaches to construction can work and work well. A book looking at Wright's construction and detailing methods and evaluating how well they worked would be most helpful – perhaps the Frank Lloyd Wright Building Conservancy, as an active recording archive of materials and information, could be of service in this respect.

Such is the curiosity about these apparently strange buildings that tours are extremely popular. Two sources for information about these events exist. The first is the Frank Lloyd Wright Building Conservancy's quarterly newsletter and their Internet site. Another reliable source of information about events, particularly special events involving their own sites, is the Frank Lloyd Wright Foundation's publication, *The Frank Lloyd Wright Quarterly*. However, a register for owners and pilgrims to co-ordinate visits and tours would be extremely worthwhile, and an inquiries service would relieve owners of the burden of answering constant queries, as well as establishing the level of interest in each building. Perhaps scholars interested in certain aspects of a building could group their visits in order to further relieve the burden on the owners.

It is the owners who are the caretakers of Wright's built legacy, and we owe them our gratitude for respecting Wright's original intentions while adapting the buildings to fit their own needs. It might be worthwhile for local gardening clubs to learn about the landscaping materials and layouts advocated by Wright, Walter Burley Griffin and Wilhelm Miller, all of whom provided planting plans for Wright buildings of the Prairie years. Teams of students from local universities could rake leaves or plant bulbs in the fall in exchange for a tour of the house. Ideas such as these could benefit both the owners and those who assist in the maintenance of the properties.

■ Frank Lloyd Wright designed his buildings to be lived in and experienced in person, not to be seen in drawings and photographs. This series of Field Guides will help locate the buildings so that they may be enjoyed first hand.

I am not at all convinced that all that we see in these buildings was consciously considered by Wright during the development of the design. When asked the source of his designs, Wright simply said 'I just shake them out of my sleeve'. When asked what his favorite project was, he said 'the next one' – giving an indication of his own outlook. Wright never felt any building was complete, he believed all of them could be improved with a new idea.

It is amazing that previously unrecorded Wright buildings are still being discovered, more than thirty-five years after his death in 1959. In early 1996, a student from the School of the Art at the Institute of Chicago discovered two in Gary, Indiana, and is now documenting them with the support of several archival sources which concentrate on Wright's work.

Approximately four hundred of Wright's buildings still stand – more if one counts garages, barns, windmills, gates, fountains and so forth. To arrive at an exact figure is difficult because what should be included as a 'Wright building', and what should not, is a matter of opinion.

Designing these buildings was not just the work of a single architect and Wright employed a staff of assistants. Some of the buildings attributed to him were drawn-up by others, although the initial designs always emanated from Wright. This Field Guide encompasses all the 'borderline' buildings which have traditionally been included in his œuvre.

During the 1950s many of the buildings in the upper Great Lakes region were featured in popular home design magazines such as *House Beautiful* and *House & Home*. The articles approached the buildings in terms of their particular features which made life easier and more enjoyable, often concentrating on the 'ranch' style homes with low pitched roofs, wide eaves and other such characteristics. Few modern amenities were incorporated in the designs of that era and are still lacking today.

In driving through neighborhoods to see these treasures, one is struck by how dull and limited the rest of the architecture is, and by the contrast between these uninspired buildings and the Wright designs. A little considerate and imaginative design could invest many otherwise standard buildings with interest, and provide some evidence of intelligence at work. Perhaps the public have been too accepting of what has been offered, but it would be good to see at least some new housing with features such as those in these Wright examples. Particularly worth studying for this purpose would be the Jacobs I and II houses, Lovness Cottage, Goetsch-Winkler House, Turkel House, Bogk House and Brauner House.

Wright's use of context should also be studied. The Olfelt, Alpaugh, Wiley, Pew, Jacobs I, Palmer and Hardy houses are all outstanding examples of the placement of buildings on site, an area at which Wright particularly excelled. The buildings were not merely placed in the center of a rectangle, but married to their location, often on difficult sites, in a way that benefits both architecture and environment.

The upper Great Lakes states are renowned for their agricultural produce: Michigan for fruits; Wisconsin for dairy produce; and Minnesota for wheat. They are also popular vacation states, with numerous rivers and lakes providing picturesque tree-lined streets and dramatic sites for houses.

There are very few early Wright buildings in the upper Great Lakes region except in Wisconsin, the land of Wright's ancestors and his birthplace. However, overall a quarter of Wright's built designs are concentrated in these three northern states. The best and most important of all of Wright's work is Taliesin, located in southwest Wisconsin. Aspects of Taliesin are also to be found in a great many of his other buildings in this region.

There are more Wright-designed housing groups in this region than in any other. Many of these are based on co-operatives. Galesburg and Kalamazoo have remained closest to their original intention but the Okemos work comes in a close third. Whitehall was a speculative project and the houses at Delavan Lake were developed by a loose association of Wright's neighbors from Chicago. There are also many examples of two houses near or next to each other in the same town. It seems it often took the combined courage or interest of two families to go ahead and build.

The ideals of progressive education are expressed in the Hillside I and II buildings, which became Wright's School for the Allied Arts in the late 1920s, and was later reorganized into the Taliesin Fellowship. This interest in the ideal of a well-rounded education came initially from Wright's aunts, Nell and Jane. His own experience at his Oak Park studio evolved into the programs which continue to grow at Taliesin and Taliesin West. The school Wright founded at Spring Green was in part a reaction to Saarinen's Cranbrook schools at Bloomfield Hills, Michigan. The architectural education outlined and promoted by both Saarinen and Wright was developed in part from the studio ideas of HH Richardson in the 1870s and 1880s in Boston.

The people who commissioned Wright buildings were considered by many to be middle class. All the houses are approximately 2,000 square feet in size and are located on modest urban or suburban lots. Many of his clients were teachers or were associated with universities. Few were wealthy business people and only Johnson, Heurtley and Waller could be considered very wealthy.

Wright's examples of production dwellings for the masses, such as the precut Richards House and the Erdman Prefabs, are well represented in the upper Great Lakes region. His earliest experiments of 1911, the American Systems Buildings, began with an association between Wright and the Richards brothers of Milwaukee. The Madison architect and contractor, Marshall Erdman, developed a line of prefabricated buildings in the 1950s which were Wright's last example of mass-produced housing. Neither of these projects was a runaway financial success. In the past five years many previously unknown buildings from these two series have come to our attention.

The three religious buildings, the Unity Chapel, the Unitarian Meeting House, and the

Annunciation Greek Orthodox Church, remind us with their different designs of the diversity of Wright's approach. The 1886 Unity Chapel at Spring Green by Joseph Silsbee was the first architectural project Wright was involved in. The other churches were designed near the end of his life, in the 1950s.

Nautical buildings play a big role in this region, with boathouses for individuals and municipalities; Jones Boathouse, Municipal Boathouse, Rockyroost, Yahara Boat Club and Monona Terrace are all in southern Wisconsin, mostly in the Madison area. Again, the variety of design solutions that Wright brings to these projects would be unexpected for any designer other than Wright.

Summer and vacation homes abound in this region. Wright's many summer houses reflect the casual vacation lifestyle. These buildings were plain and unornamented but not uninteresting. All are modest in size and scale. Even the Heurtley Cottage is modest, considering that it was built in a neighborhood whose inhabitants included the McCormicks, Fords and Firestones at Marquette Island.

Wright's Background

Wright was born in Richland Center, Wisconsin, on 8 June 1867, just two years after the end of the Civil War. Due to lack of documentation his exact birthplace is unknown. During his boyhood the family moved to nearby McGregor, Iowa, and then to central Madison, Wisconsin. As a boy, Wright spent many summers helping on the farms of his mother's family in the Jones Valley, just south of Spring Green. He went to elementary school and high school in Madison and attended the engineering program at the University of Wisconsin, but did not graduate. At the age of nineteen he decided to pursue his dream of becoming an architect by moving to Chicago where he found work with Joseph Silsbee, who was a friend of his Unitarian minister uncle, Jenkin Lloyd Jones. He later joined the progressive firm of architects, Adler & Sullivan. In 1893, after a dispute about work undertaken by Wright outside the firm, he set up his own practice, where his first client was Herman Winslow of River Forest.

He married nineteen-year-old Catherine Tobin in 1889 and they had six children in their new home in Oak Park. Two of these children, Lloyd and John, became architects. Lloyd (Frank Lloyd Wright, Jr) designed the first Hollywood Bowl, and John was the inventor of Lincoln Logs, the children's toy. His granddaughter, Anne Baxter, became a well-known Hollywood actress and his two youngest sons constructed houses designed for them by their father.

Wright's architectural output may be organized into four distinct periods. The earliest, from 1889 to 1900, is often referred to as pre-Prairie. These buildings vary widely in form but all have an inventiveness that distinguishes them from other architecture of the time. Included in this period are most of the houses at Delavan.

In the first years of the twentieth century, from around 1900 to 1915, Wright found a visual style that was consistent without being formulaic. Buildings from this period are known as the Prairie designs, and Wright referred to the lines and colors of the Mid-western prairie when describing them. While these terms could apply to all of Wright's work, the

Prairie buildings had simple, low pitched roofs with wide overhangs. Long groups of windows were tucked under the roofs. Outstanding examples from this period include the Willits, Martin and Robie houses, Unity Temple and the Larkin Building. Some of Wright's finest designs in art glass and furniture are also from this period.

In 1909, although his architectural practice was expanding, Wright apparently felt he had to change things. He abandoned his Oak Park family, closed his office, turned over his work to another architect and left for Europe with one of his client's wives, Mamah Borthwick Cheney. His stay in Europe included trips to his publisher's office in Berlin, and time in Florence spent completing the drafting of plates for the Wasmuth Edition with his son Lloyd. He was gone nearly two years in total.

Upon his return in 1911, he decided to move to the country and chose his mother's family land, Jones Valley, as the site for Taliesin. Mamah Cheney joined him at Taliesin and he restarted his practice. Several important jobs came in soon after his return, including Midway Gardens, The Imperial Hotel, and a series of designs for the Richards Brothers' American Systems houses. The years between 1911 and the mid-1930s are often referred to as the 'lost years' and it is difficult to give a stylistic label to the work of this period because of its variety.

This was a time of turmoil in Wright's personal and professional life. In 1914 Mamah and her two children were murdered and Taliesin was set on fire. Several years after the tragedy, he married Miriam Noel, a marriage soon to be beset with problems. Damage caused by fires in both 1914 and 1925 were, amongst other things, the cause of the financial problems that made him leave Taliesin and settle in Los Angeles for a time. During this turmoil he met Olga Lasovitch, whom he married after his divorce from Miriam Noel in the late 1920s.

Once the difficulties with Miriam Noel had passed, life improved. Olga adopted the name Olgivanna and had another child, Iovanna, with Wright. Olgivanna convinced him to write the story of his life, which was published in 1932. After reading it, Edgar Kaufmann, Jr, persuaded his father to hire Wright to design a weekend house in the mountains outside Pittsburgh. This house we now know as Fallingwater. The notoriety of the autobiography led Herbert Johnson of Racine to ask Wright to design the new Administration Building for Johnson Wax. The combination of these commissions launched Wright into a successful second career that lasted from the 1930s until his death in 1959.

In 1937, Wright was seventy years old. Many might think this is too old to embark upon a renaissance, but at eighty-eight Wright designed the Guggenheim Museum, New York, and at ninety the Marin County Civic Center, as well as hundreds of houses in the intervening years.

Not only did his architectural career revive but, with Olgivanna, he founded a school for architects that continues today, the Taliesin Fellowship. There is no doubt that Olgivanna's influence contributed to Wright's career renaissance: within a few years of their marriage Wright was involved in the second wave of genius and designed the Johnson Wax Administration Building and Fallingwater. The ideas and designs that were 'shaken out of his sleeve' were not as strikingly ornate as those of the Prairie years but they were in many ways more innovative architecturally. Wright made a concerted effort to design housing for minimal budgets, for instance, with the two beautiful and significant houses for Herbert Jacobs. Herbert Jacobs put him to the test on two occasions and succeeded beautifully. Wright seems to have relished challenges, and would deliver in difficult circumstances. Many other clients who received unexpectedly expensive solutions did not return to Wright demanding economy as Jacobs did, they include Scully, Marcus and others.

Some of the Usonian Houses seem to be designed to a formula but, with different site conditions and climates, the Jacobs, Smith, and Rosenbaum houses are all quite different in feel. The Jacobs house has an experimental feel, while the MM Smith House is very refined. Even comparing the hemicycles of the Jacobs and Meyer houses gives one an appreciation of the individuality of each building.

Wright lived for almost ninety-two years. During his lifetime indoor plumbing became commonplace, the radio, television and telephone were invented and, by 1959, nearly every household in the United States had one of each. In 1867, the year of Wright's birth, there were only thirty-seven states in the Union, and there was no trans-continental railroad until 1869. It was over thirty years from Wright's birth until Henry Ford and the Wright brothers began to produce automobiles and airplanes. Two years before Wright's death, the Russians launched the Sputnik satellite and the Space Age was begun. This was quite a time in history. By the time of Frank Lloyd Wright's death, the world little resembled the one into which he had been born.

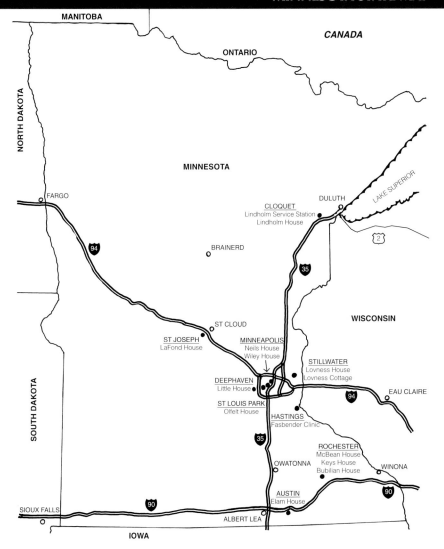

MANITOBA

CANADA

ONTARIO

NORTH DAKOTA

MINNESOTA

FARGO

DULUTH

LAKE SUPERIOR

CLOQUET
Lindholm Service Station
Lindholm House

94

BRAINERD

35

ST CLOUD

WISCONSIN

ST JOSEPH
LaFond House

MINNEAPOLIS
Neils House
Wiley House

STILLWATER
Lovness House
Lovness Cottage

SOUTH DAKOTA

DEEPHAVEN
Little House

EAU CLAIRE

94

ST LOUIS PARK
Olfelt House

HASTINGS
Fasbender Clinic

35

ROCHESTER
McBean House
Keys House
Bubilian House

OWATONNA

WINONA

90

AUSTIN
Elam House

SIOUX FALLS

90

ALBERT LEA

IOWA

■ Minnesota is known as the 'Land of Ten Thousand Lakes', and it is thus no surprise that the majority of Wright's buildings here were constructed on lake shores. However, Wright's sensitivity to local environmental conditions is not as apparent in these buildings as it is in those designed for desert climates. For instance, although more snow falls here than in most parts of the country, the roof pitch and overhangs do not reflect this. Most of the designs in Minnesota are located in the southeast quadrant of the state, where the greatest population is centered.

LINDHOLM SERVICE STATION
202 Cloquet Avenue
Cloquet, Minnesota 55720
1957   5739

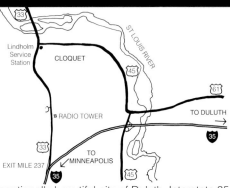

Directions: Cloquet is west of the exceptionally beautiful city of Duluth. Interstate 35 connects Minneapolis and Duluth. Exit at mile 237 and take Highway 33 north for 1.5 miles. The service station is located at the southeast corner of Route 45 and Highway 33, next to the Post Office and before the bridge over the St Louis River.

Accessibility: The station can be seen at all times and in all conditions. However, there is little to recommend a trip so far north unless visiting Duluth or the Boundary Waters.

■ Wright wanted to improve the appearance of this ugly service station which he became aware of driving back and forth between Arizona and Wisconsin. This explains why the second floor and cantilever appear to be additions to a standard rectangular concrete block service station. Although originally the building contained many innovative features, developed during the late 1920s, most of them are not permissible under today's environmental standards, for instance, the hoses no longer hang from above. Unfortunately the station has not been well maintained, looking better in photographs than reality, and the second-floor office is no longer used.

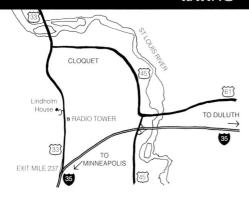

RW LINDHOLM HOUSE
Route 33
Cloquet, Minnesota 55720
1952   5208

Directions: Similar to the Lindholm Service Station. Exit Interstate 35 north on Highway 33 and continue for 0.9 miles where the driveway is located to the west, just north of the radio tower. It is not marked and divides almost immediately with the gate to the house located to the north. There is a sign on the gate which states Mantyla.

Accessibility: The house cannot be seen from the street and is difficult to locate.

■ Built a few years before the service station, this house is constructed from concrete blocks on a site that slopes steeply to the west. The layout and the roof are not noticeably different to the majority of houses Wright built in the early 1950s, which is probably due to the extreme weather conditions typical of its northern locale.

DR EDWARD LAFOND HOUSE
29710 Kipper Road
St Joseph, Minnesota 56374
1960   5518

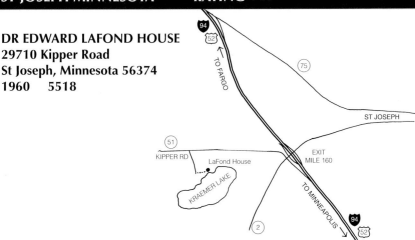

Directions: The LaFond House is not actually in St Joseph but is in fact west of Interstate 94. At mile 160 Exit 94 to the south (about 200 feet) and proceed west on Highway 51 about a mile to Kipper Road. The house is just to the northwest on Kraemer Lake.

Accessibility: Cannot be seen from public property.

■ This is one of the last of the Erdman Prefabs. The scheme was initiated after Dr LaFond, who was having a medical prefab built, learned about the Wright designs and commissioned the house through Erdman's company. Suprisingly the client never contacted Wright or Taliesin. The client's brother was the carpenter for this project. It is in perfect original condition except for a sliding glass door designed and approved recently by the Taliesin Associated Architects.

PAUL OLFELT HOUSE
2206 Parklands Lane
St Louis Park, Minnesota 55416
1958   5820

Directions: Difficult to describe. Southeast of the intersection of Interstate 394/Route 12 and Highway 100, north of Twin Lakes and south of the Burlington Northern RR tracks. The streets turn and change names rapidly, so be careful and watch for street numbers to tell how close it is. Cedarwood runs along the north shore of Twin Lakes and connects Parkwoods Road to the west with Parklands Road to the east. Parklands Road runs north-south for about two blocks. Toward the north of this short street, past Forest Road, Parklands Lane veers to the northwest. The house is located at the end of this lane on the south side of the cul-de-sac. Just east of Parklands Road is another north-south road with several names: France Avenue, Ewing Avenue and further north to 394/12 it becomes the end of Cedar Lake Parkway.

Accessibility: Only the street facade is visible. The private sides are not accessible.

■ A very good building, completed a year after Wright's death; typical of his later urban houses but often overlooked. The residence is very small although it appears larger when viewed from the street. The slit windows provide privacy without obstructing views.

HENRY J NEILS HOUSE
2801 Burnham Boulevard
Minneapolis, Minnesota 55416
1950 5020

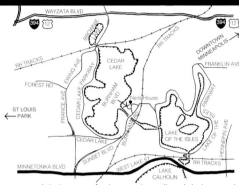

Directions: This house is not difficult to get to, it is just confusing to describe. It is located on the southeast shore of Cedar Lake on the west side of Minneapolis. Take Highway 100 and exit to the east on Route 7 which becomes Sunset Boulevard. Burnham Road intersects Sunset approximately two blocks after the roadway becomes a street. Take Burnham Road northeast and continue for another block, over a small bridge, where Burnham Boulevard is located to the west. Watch for the house numbers once on the Boulevard.

(From time to time the Minneapolis Institute of Arts displays its fragments of the Little House. The Institute is east of the Neils House and Interstate 35W and 94. There are many great Purcell & Elmslie houses in this neighborhood.)

Accessibility: Visible from street all year round, and the park to the rear during winter.

■ This house, designed for a stone distributor, is unusual even for Wright as the typical wood details are missing, the mullions are aluminium, and the living room ceiling is pitched and very high. The house overlooks Cedar Lake to the northwest. Neils' daughter married Cedric Boulter who built a Wright-designed house in Cincinnati (see East volume).

MALCOM E WILEY HOUSE
255 Bedford Street, SE
Minneapolis, Minnesota 55414
1933   3401

Directions: The house is tucked in at the south end of Bedford Street, two blocks south of Franklin Avenue, just east of Interstate 94/Highway 12 and west of Route 280. It is almost on the eastern border of Minneapolis and north of the Mississippi River.

Accessibility: During the winter months there are glimpses of the house through the foliage in front of the living room and the bedrooms, but venturing closer would be intrusive.

■ This is the first Usonian House constructed, and while it is not typical of those built later it is a masterpiece nonetheless. This was the first house by Wright to have the kitchen joined to the living and dining areas – described by Wright as a 'workspace'. The furniture designed for this house is as important as the architecture. The client, Mr Wiley, was an economist and later became a Dean at the university a few blocks away. The house has recently been restored, the interior and brick terrace in particular.

DONALD LOVNESS HOUSE
10121 83rd Street North
Stillwater, Minnesota 55082
1955   5507

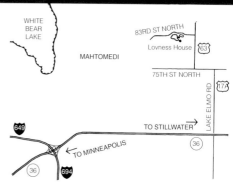

Directions: Located between Stillwater and Mahtomedi, east of St Paul and north of Route 36. Exit 36 at Lake Elmo Road. Take 17A north and turn west on 75th Street North and continue for 0.5 miles to Kimbro/Highway 63. Take Kimbro/Highway 63 north. Turn onto 83rd Street North and continue for 0.8 miles. Turn west onto a small drive to the north of Woodpile Lake and continue for 0.5 miles.

Accessibility: The compound is not accessible because of the narrow private road and the ferocious animals kept by the owners. Unless invited, it would be better to avoid this house.

■ This is one of the most innovative houses designed by Wright in the fifties, due to the exceptional relationship between the clients and the staff at Taliesin. The house has only three rooms, discounting bathrooms, yet achieves a high degree of privacy. The height of the living room is not extreme but appears greater than usual. The dining table promotes intimacy while remaining a part of the larger space. The entire house was built by Mr and Mrs Lovness while they lived in a small trailer on the property.

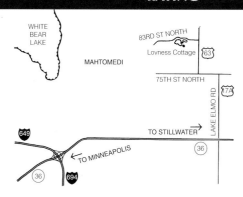

WHITE BEAR LAKE

MAHTOMEDI

83RD ST NORTH

Lovness Cottage   63

75TH ST NORTH

LAKE ELMO RD

17A

649

TO STILLWATER →

← TO MINNEAPOLIS

36

694

36

DONALD LOVNESS COTTAGE
10121 83rd Street North
Stillwater, Minnesota 55082
1974   5824

Directions: Located between Stillwater and Mahtomedi, east of St Paul and north of Route 36. Exit 36 at Lake Elmo Road. Take 17A north and turn west on 75th Street North and continue for 0.5 miles to Kimbro/Highway 63. Take Kimbro/Highway 63 north. Turn onto 83rd Street North and continue for 0.8 miles. Turn west onto a small drive to the north of Woodpile Lake and continue for 0.5 miles.

Accessibility: The compound is not accessible because of the narrow private road and ferocious animals kept by the owners. Unless invited, it would be better to avoid this house.

■ This cottage – one of several designed at Mrs Lovness' request – is much better constructed than the Peterson Cottage (p37) to which it is almost identical. Mr Lovness made all of the casework and furniture for both house and cottage. Extra chairs from the cottage are now in museum collections.

FASBENDER MEDICAL CLINIC
801 Pine Street at Highway 55
Hastings, Minnesota 55033
1957   5730

Directions: Hastings is southeast of Minneapolis on the Mississippi River. Route 55 connects Minneapolis and Hastings and enters the town as 8th Street. The Clinic is easy to find and is located to the west at the corner of Pine and 8th Street, just east of the High School.

Accessibility: Open to the public but no tours given.

■ The recently restored copper roof, almost touching the ground, gives this building a presence that is unexpected and provides an excellent opportunity to observe Wright's approach to small projects. The medical practice moved out years ago and the clinic has had a variety of tenants since then. Thankfully the owners have maintained the original design.

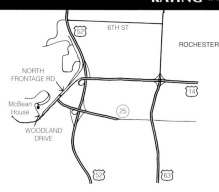

JAMES B McBEAN HOUSE
1532 Woodland Drive, SW
Rochester, Minnesota 55901
1957   5706

Directions: This can be confusing. Located in southwest Rochester, 100 feet southwest of the Highway 14 and Highway 52 intersection. Exit 14 westbound along North Frontage Road for one block (0.2 miles) turning north along Woodland Drive. Follow this road up the hill and around the curve to 1532. (Highway 52 forms a barrier to this neighborhood and can only be crossed here at Highway 14, and further north at 6th street.)

(The Keys (p28) and Bubilian houses (p29) are further along North Frontage Road eastbound. TJ Maxx Plaza and Apache Mall can be found to the east of these houses.)

Accessibility: Visible from the street and in very good condition.

■ This box-like two-story Erdman Prefab is located on a sloping site and seems uncomfortable there. Despite this the position of the house provides a spectacular view from the living room. Very little is known about the McBeans.

THOMAS E KEYS HOUSE
1243 Skyline Drive
Rochester, Minnesota 55901
1950   5012

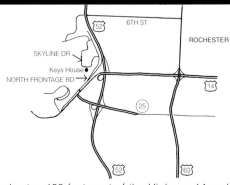

Directions: Located in southwest Rochester, 100 feet west of the Highway 14 and Highway 52 intersection. Exit 14 westbound along North Frontage Road for one block (0.2 miles) turning west along Skyline Drive. Follow this road up the hill to 1243. (Highway 52 forms a barrier to this neighborhood and can only be crossed at Highway 14 and further north at 6th Street.)

(The McBean (p27) and Bubilian houses (p29) are also located along North Frontage Road, while TJ Maxx Plaza and Apache Mall can be found to the east of these houses.)

Accessibility: Visible from the street to the north.

■ This house was based on a co-operative housing scheme for Detroit, designed in 1938 and described by Wright in *Architectural Forum,* which was never realized due to a lack of cooperation. An earth berm to the north and windows to the south are used to improve the dwelling's thermal performance. The only other design to use an earth berm as insulation is Herbert Jacobs' Solar Hemicycle (pp54-55). This structure appears quite small from the street but much larger from the garden.

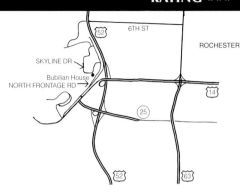

AH BUBILIAN HOUSE
1229 Skyline Drive
Rochester, Minnesota 55901
1947   4709

Directions: Located in southwest Rochester, 100 feet west of the Highway 14 and Highway 52 intersection. Exit 14 westbound along North Frontage Road for one block (0.2 miles) turning west along Skyline Drive. Follow this road up the hill to 1229. (Highway 52 forms a barrier to this neighborhood and can only be crossed at Highway 14 and further north at 6th Street.)

(The McBean (p27) and Keys houses (p28) are also located along North Frontage Road, while TJ Maxx Plaza and Apache Mall can be found to the east of these houses.)

Accessibility: Not visible from the street.

■ Wright's mastery of site planning is evident here. The offset living and dining rooms break the composition's strict rectangularity and enhance the view to the southeast. The original clients lived in this house longer than most others, from the 1940s till the 1990s. Financial savings were achieved by altering the standard materials and methods used in the basic wall construction.

SP ELAM HOUSE
309 21st St SW
Austin, Minnesota 55912
1951   5105

[Map showing the location of the Elam House in Austin, Minnesota, with streets labeled: 14TH ST, AUSTIN, 90, OAKLAND ST, Elam House, 3RD AVE, AIRPORT, 90, 22ND ST, 21ST ST, 17TH ST]

Directions: Austin is south of Minneapolis near the Iowa border and east of Interstate 35. Interstate 90 runs east-west to the north of the town. The house is located to the west, just south of Austin's main thoroughfare, Oakland Street, in the Elam neighborhood where the streets are gently curved, breaking the town's rigid grid. Third Avenue runs east and meets 21st Street. The house is positioned near the corner.
(In nearby Owatonna is a wonderful Louis Sullivan bank on the main square.)

Accessibility: Visible and comprehensible from the street.

■ The Elam House is one of the largest later Usonian Houses, and is only surpassed by Johnson's Wingspread house in Racine. The entrance is located at the lowest level providing access to the living room in the center of the east wing via a staircase. Only a three bedroom house, it appears much larger.

DULUTH
CLOQUET

LAKE SUPERIOR

LAKE SUPERIOR

MICHIGAN

MARQUETTE

35

2

41 28

41 28

2

41

51

← TO MINNEAPOLIS

94

WAUSAU
Manson House
Wright House

MINNESOTA

PLOVER
Iber House

GREEN
BAY

LAKE MICHIGAN

90

51

OSHKOSH
Hunt Bungalow

141

TWO RIVERS
Schwartz House
WAUWATOSA
Greek Orthodox
Church
BAYSIDE
Mollica House
FOX POINT
Adelman House
MILWAUKEE
Richards Duplex Apts
Small House
Bungalow
Munkwitz Duplex
Bogk House
WIND POINT
Johnson House
(Wingspread)
RACINE
Keland House
Johnson Wax Co
Hardy House
DOUSMAN
Greenberg House

LACROSSE

BEAVER DAM
Jackson House

41

151

LAKE DELTON
Peterson Cottage

IOWA

MADISON
Jacobs I House
Gilmore House
Nautical Buildings
Lamp House
Van Tamlen House
Rudin House

RICHLAND CENTER
German Warehouse

14

MIDDLETON
Jacobs II House

LANCASTER
Kinney House

COLUMBUS
Arnold House

IXONIA

94

SHOREWOOD HILLS
Pew House
Unitarian Meeting House

JEFFERSON
Smith House

90

67

LAKE
GENEVA

151

DUBUQUE

SPRING GREEN
Taliesin
Visitors' Center
Hillside School
Midway Barns
Porter House
Romeo and Juliet Windmill
Unity Chapel
Wyoming Valley School

ILLINOIS

ROCKFORD
Laurent House

BELVIDERE
Pettit Chapel

94

12

DELAVAN
Spencer House
Ross House
Jones Gatehouse
Jones House
Wallis Cottage
Johnson House

90

CHICAGO

■ Approximately half of all Wright's buildings in the Upper Great Lakes are located in southern Wisconsin. Wright spent more time in this state than anywhere else: he was born here; grew up here; attended the University of Wisconsin in Madison; and was eventually buried here. His mother's family, the Lloyd Jones, first settled in the village of Ixonia, just west of Milwaukee, in the mid-1800s (although the precise location has yet to be identified), and then moved to what is now known as the Jones Valley, south of Spring Green. After Wright returned to his family's homestead, there were many troubles at Taliesin – including two fires, the murder of several people, and financial difficulties – which caused life to be anything but tranquil. The financing of the property was in similar turmoil, with different individuals and institutions making claims on the estate, forcing Wright to live elsewhere. The maintenance of the buildings during these years was unfortunately neglected, and as a result they are far more difficult to restore.

CHARLES L MANSON HOUSE
1224 Highland Park Boulevard
Wausau, Wisconsin 54401
1940   4009

Directions: Located in northeast Wausau. Exit Highway 51 at mile 192 east on Stewart, continuing into town. Take 5th or 6th Street north to Franklin and proceed east. Then proceed north on 10th Street to Highland Park Boulevard. The house is to the east, on the north side of the street down the slope from the road. (It should be noted that the city has no through streets.)

Accessibility: Visible from street and backyard but little to see.

■ This is an unusual house that has very few windows but great views. Originally access appears to have been located to the rear of the house. The hallway connects this entrance with the living room and bisects the bedrooms. There are tall windows and doors in the east and south walls of the living room, but they do not engender the sense of openness typical of Usonian Houses.

DUEY WRIGHT HOUSE
904 Grand Avenue
Wausau, Wisconsin 54401
1957   5727

Directions: This house is hard to find and is easily missed in a car. It is located south of the downtown area, between the railroad and a series of brick apartment houses on the west side of Grand Avenue. It is just south of Thomas, and three-and-a-half blocks north of Town Line Road on the east bank of the Wisconsin River.

Accessibility: The house can only be approached via the long driveway and by the time the house becomes visible one is nearly at the front door.

■ Duey Wright owned a music store in Wausau and his family now runs the local radio station (they are not related to the architect, however). It is one of the few Wright houses with a specific music room opposite the entrance. The living room provides views of the Wisconsin River and on a clear day Rib Mountain can be seen. Like the Wiley house (p23), this residence has no specific dining room, and the kitchen overlooks the drive and front yard. At the south end of the kitchen there is a space for eating.

FRANK IBER HOUSE
3000 Springville Drive
Plover, Wisconsin 54467
1957   5518

Directions: Plover is south of Stevens Point just west of Business 51. Springville Drive is 1.2 miles north of Route B/Route 54, and is located in close proximity to the south bank of the Little Plover River in the block between Business 51 and the railroad tracks to the west. The Iber house is on the northeast corner.

Accessibility: Visible through fence.

■ This property is now enclosed by chain-link fencing and the features that are usually associated with the Erdman Prefabs cannot be easily seen. The two-story main wing faces to the east. The landscaping on the large lot is extensive and well developed.

STEPHEN MB HUNT BUNGALOW
1165 Algoma Boulevard
Oshkosh, Wisconsin 54901
1917   1703

Directions: Oshkosh is on the west shore of Lake Winnebago. The Hunt house is located just south of the intersection of New York Avenue and Algoma Boulevard. It is one block south of Route 21, Oshkosh Avenue, which is an exit off Highway 41. It is just north of the Fox River.

(Oshkosh is the site of an annual experimental air show held at the beginning of August.)

Accessibility: Visible from the street.

■ It appears that this is another example of the precut houses marketed by the Richards Company of Milwaukee. However, the drawings with a Frank Lloyd Wright title block include a landscape design by his son Lloyd Wright. Others of this type can be found in Milwaukee (p82) and in the northern suburbs of Chicago (see MetroChicago volume). Previously Mr Hunt had commissioned Wright to design a house for him in LaGrange, a suburb west of Chicago. The art glass in this residence is more elaborate than other precut buildings. It is unusual to see such a modest building in a neighborhood of much larger houses.

BERNARD SCHWARTZ HOUSE
3425 Adams Street
Two Rivers, Wisconsin 54241
1939   3904

Directions: Two Rivers is 6 miles northeast of Manitowoc on the shore of Lake Michigan. The house is north of downtown at the intersection of Adams Street and 34th Street. There are two major routes into town off Interstate 43. The first is at mile 154 east Route 310 which crosses the West River at 14th. The house is just after the junction with 34th Street on the opposite side of the road. The secondary route to the house is further north at mile 164 Interstate 43. Exit 43 at Highway 147 east for 7 miles, turning southeast on 34th Street for one block and finally east to Adams Street continuing for one block.

Accessibility: Visible from street, but visibility reduced by trees.

■ This early Usonian House was based on a home designed for a family with a $5,000 to $6,000 income which appeared in a 1938 *Life* magazine article. It overlooks the East Twin River. The internal and external finishes are red brick and brown wood, a combination that creates a striking contrast. Mr Schwartz, who ran a small textile business, built the house in 1939 for $18,000.

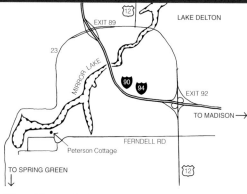

SETH PETERSON COTTAGE
E 9982 Ferndell Road
Lake Delton, Wisconsin 53940
1958   5821

Directions: On Interstate 90/94 take Exit 92 south for 1 mile. Turn onto Ferndell Road and travel west for 2.5 miles, following the curve. The Peterson Cottage is on a gravel road north of Ferndell Road.
(The Ho-Chunk Casino is 2.3 miles south of Ferndell Road.)

Accessibility: Public tours are given on the second Sunday of each month from 1 to 4pm. Private tours on Sundays and vacation rental can also be arranged. Contact: Seth Peterson Cottage Conservancy, PO Box 334, Lake Delton, Wisconsin 53940; rentals 608-254-6551, though this should be done well in advance.

■ Mr Peterson, a computer programer, commissioned this building in 1957 though he never lived in it as he committed suicide before it was complete. The cottage, a duplicate of the Lovness Cottage (p25), remained derelict for years until it was restored by Audrey Laatsch in the 1990s. The 880-square-foot house has an excellent view of Mirror Lake over to the southwest.

PATRICK KINNEY HOUSE
474 North Filmore Street
Lancaster, Wisconsin 53813
1951   5038

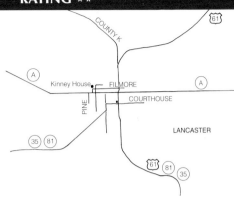

Directions: Located in the northwest corner of Lancaster, several blocks west of Highway 61. The town is laid out in a simple grid, with the east-west streets named after trees and the north-south streets named after the presidents of the United States. The Kinney house is located at the northwest corner of the intersection of Filmore (the 13th president) and Pine.

(Just northwest of Lancaster, on the western bank of the Mississippi River at the end of the Wisconsin River, is McGregor, Iowa, where Wright and his family lived for a short time when he was a boy.)

Accessibility: Only the carport and beautiful stone wall are visible from the street.

■ A pleasant house that has few flourishes apart from the view to the northwest. Like Donald Lovness (p24), Mr Kinney, an attorney, acted as his own contractor and even quarried much of the stone himself to save on construction costs. The house is a single-story construction at grade.

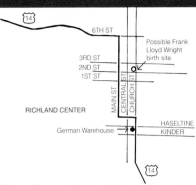

ALBERT D GERMAN WAREHOUSE
300 South Church Street
Richland Center, Wisconsin 53581
1915   1504

Directions: Richland Center is on Route 14, about 30 miles west of Spring Green. Route 14, or Church Street, cuts through the town. It does a zigzag through the grid. If entering town from the south follow Church Street to the warehouse which is located to the west at the junction of Haseltine and Church. From the north, Route 14 is signposted one block west of Church Street. The building is between Haseltine to the north and Kinder to the south.

(Although no precise records are available, it is believed that Wright was born in the Weigley house on the northwest corner of Church and Second Streets.)

Accessibility: Reduced visibility from the street, but tours are available June-October. Contact: 608-647-2808; or Richland Center Chamber of Commerce: 800-422-1318.

■ This is a great building. The design is evocative of ancient Mexican architecture, although the exact inspiration is unimportant. Since the collapse of the original owner's company during the Great Depression, this warehouse has had a variety of uses but fortunately it is still in good condition.

TALIESIN MAP, SPRING GREEN

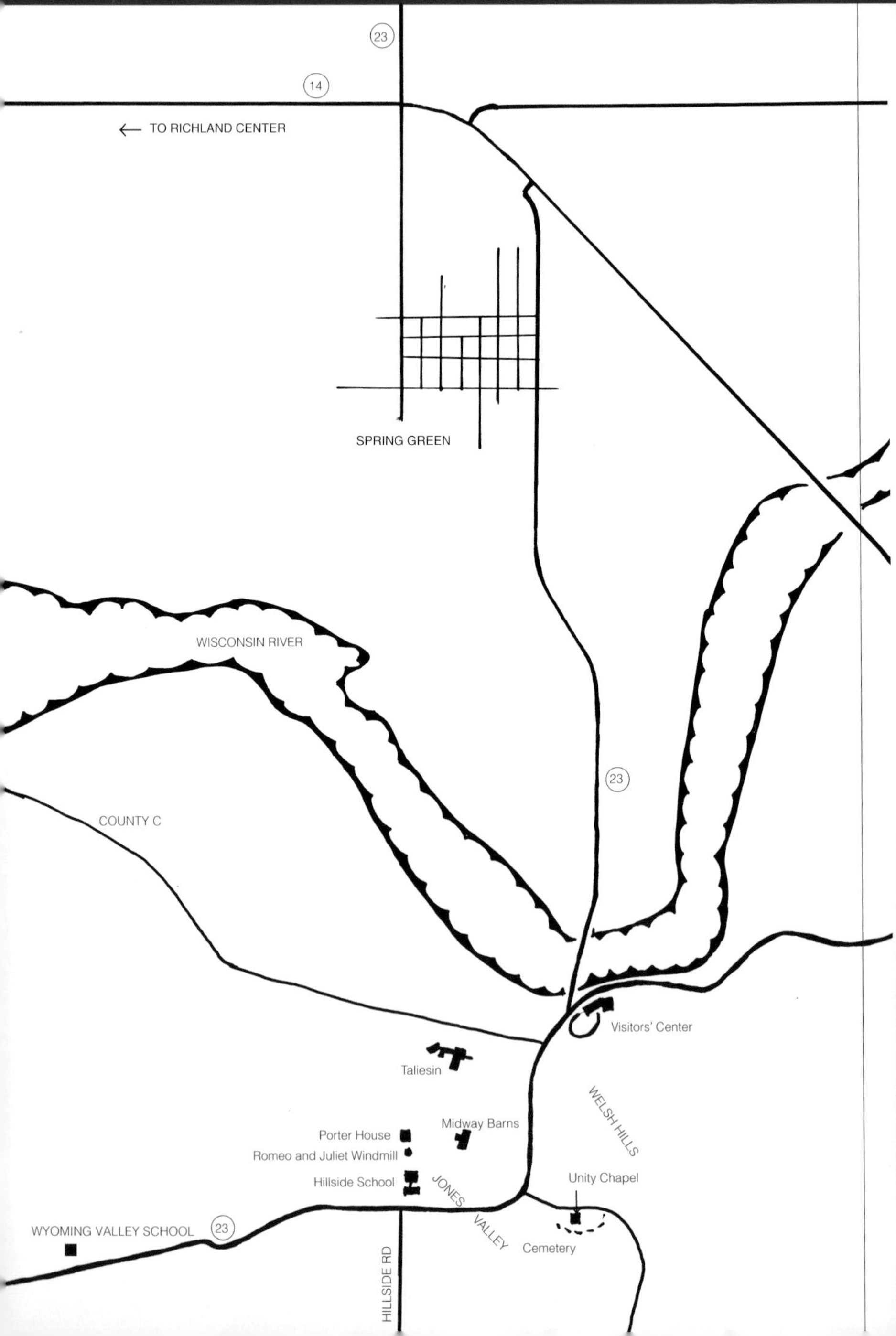

23
14
TO RICHLAND CENTER
SPRING GREEN
WISCONSIN RIVER
23
COUNTY C
Visitors' Center
Taliesin
WELSH HILLS
Midway Barns
Porter House
Romeo and Juliet Windmill
Hillside School
JONES VALLEY
Unity Chapel
WYOMING VALLEY SCHOOL
23
Cemetery
HILLSIDE RD

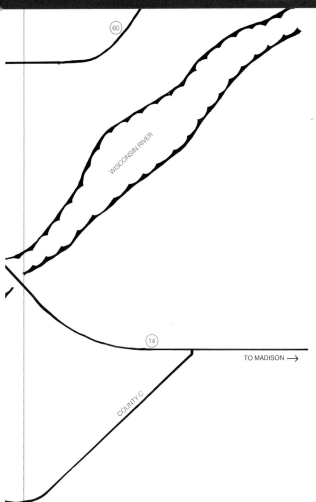

WISCONSIN RIVER

60

14

TO MADISON →

COUNTY C

■ Wright's only other building in Spring Green was not for himself or any of his family. It was the Women's Building (Opus # 1413), an exhibition pavilion at the fairgrounds. It opened in 1914, just two weeks after the fire at Taliesin, and was very similar to the Yahara Boathouse but with a narrow gable roof over the center. The date of its demolition is unknown.

The three hills across the valley to the east of Taliesin – Bryn Mawr, Bryn Canol and Bryn Bach – are referred to as the Welsh Hills. By naming his house Taliesin, Wright exhibited strong ties to his Welsh ancestry. In an 1854 English-Welsh dictionary the notation for a 'brow or edge of a hill' is 'ffring and ffrin' and the term 'brow' is defined as 'tal and talcen'. Besides the references to the bard, Taliesin, no one has located a secondary meaning for the word.

Wright altered the landscape of the valley to complement his building, a process that involved eliminating trees, fences and buildings that interfered with his design. Throughout his life Wright photographed the valley, and the surviving original photographic prints provide a rare insight into his involvement in this medium.

TALIESIN
Route 23
Spring Green, Wisconsin 53588
1911   1104

Directions: South of Spring Green on Route 23. Taliesin is the first building to the west after crossing the Wisconsin River.

Accessibility: You must visit this site at least once in your life. The building is open in the spring, summer and part of the fall, with several tour options available at the Visitors' Center – the former Riverview Terrace Restaurant (p45). Contact: The Frank Lloyd Wright Foundation, PO Box 399, Spring Green, Wisconsin 53588; information and reservations: 608-588-7900.

■ Technically, Taliesin is just this single building, though the name is now applied to the whole valley, especially the holdings of the Frank Lloyd Wright Foundation. It was built in 1911, just after Wright returned from a two year sojourn in Europe. The earliest drawings list his mother as the client, but the plan was clearly for him and Mamah Borthwick, the former Mrs Cheney, with whom he had lived in Europe. Prior to this Wright had left Catherine, his wife of twenty years, and his six children in Oak Park to start anew, scandalizing society in the process.

Taliesin is the epitome of Wright's genius and must be visited. None of his other buildings serve such complex functions, and yet retain their graceful rusticity. As Neil Levine recently stated: 'Geometry allowed the artist to seize upon the essentials and give to the image of a natural form that inner harmony which penetrates the outer form and is its determining character'. This is the organic principle which is the basis for all Wright's work.

The valley is a spectacular place. It may not have the drama of the Grand Canyon but it has just the right balance of natural and man-made elements. The spaces created between the hill and the residence make it feel as if the building is meant to be there. While it does not command the highest point in the valley, it still has expansive views.

Paralleling Wright's life in many ways, Taliesen has been in a state of continual flux since its initial construction. It is a living organism that is now being restored under the careful supervision of the Taliesin Preservation Commission.

Most of the work was planned, but there were two catastrophic events that reshaped the building and Wright's life. On the 15 August 1914 a servant set fire to the dining room killing Mamah Borthwick, her two children, and several others. At this time Wright was in Chicago with his son John supervising the construction of the Midway Gardens (now demolished). On their return to Spring Green by train they were joined by Mr Cheney who had been notified of the deaths. This was the most devastating single event in Wright's entire life. Another fire occurred in 1925 when the house was hit by lightning, and once again part of the building was destroyed. Miraculously the archive was not lost, and Wright's remarkable plans and perspectives have been preserved.

Taliesin was named after a Welsh poet and bard, as Wright's ancestors were from Wales and he always felt a deep affinity for his heritage. The three hills across the valley also have Welsh names, Bryn Mawr, Bryn Canol and Bryn Bach.

The courtyard flower garden and outdoor tearoom, with its curved stone bench under an oak tree canopy, provide the transition between the building and the crest of the hill. From this promontory, over the bedroom wing and into the valley beyond, is one of Taliesin's great views.

The living room is one of the outstanding spaces created by Wright, and is a room of complexity and variety. The inglenook contrasts superbly with the bench along the windows that overlook the valley. There are low spaces that feel comfortable when occupied by a single individual, yet the room itself feels just as warm when there are sixty people. The main dining table has always been located at the base of the tallest wall. The eastward expansion of the room took a dramatic turn when Wright acquired steel beams from the old Wisconsin River Bridge and built the cantilevered birdwalk.

The Taliesin house tour includes a visit to Wright's bedroom. Here the very low ceiling is balanced by the higher clerestory, which not only relieves the compression but illuminates what would otherwise be a dark interior. The desk in this room was often used for the preliminary drawings of many important buildings.

The property's maintenance and farming were carried out by the architectural apprentices as Wright felt that, in the attempt to understand nature, work in the fields and on the farm was as important as work at the drafting board. In contrast to this heavy and often dirty manual work was the formal entertainment held on Saturday nights. This began with a gathering for cocktails in the living room, adjourning for a special meal prepared with the bounty gathered from the fields outside. This was followed by a live dramatic or musical program performed in an appropriate space. Initially, shortly after the founding of the Fellowship in 1932, feature, foreign and experimental films were shown at the end of the evening. It was said that the finest collection of 1930s' Russian animation was contained in the Taliesin Archives.

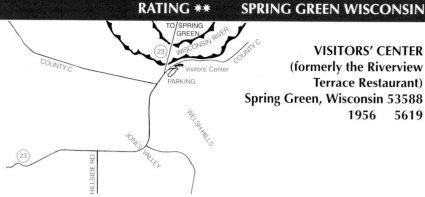

VISITORS' CENTER
(formerly the Riverview
Terrace Restaurant)
Spring Green, Wisconsin 53588
1956   5619

Directions: Located south of Route 23 and Spring Green on County C that runs along the south bank of the Wisconsin River. It is west of Tower Hill State Park.

Accessibility: Open May till October. For information and reservations contact: The Frank Lloyd Wright Foundation, PO Box 399, Spring Green, Wisconsin 53588; information and reservations: 608-588-7900.

■ Built by Karen Johnson Keland and her husband Willard Keland as a restaurant, this building is now the Visitors' Center for the Frank Lloyd Wright Foundation, containing bathrooms, book shop and food service area. The Taliesin Preservation Commission, which is overseeing the restoration of the Taliesin Valley sites, begins all tours here.

All the dining-rooms of this excellent restaurant overlooked the Wisconsin River. The west room was the lounge, with the bar in front of the windows. The floor level behind the bar was lower than the main room so that the bartenders did not obscure the patrons' view.

The Kelands also built a Wright designed house in Racine (p90).

HILLSIDE HOME SCHOOL
Route 23
Spring Green, Wisconsin 53588
1902   0216

Directions: South of Taliesin on Highway 23. Located at the intersection with Hillside Road.

Accessibility: Tours arranged through the Taliesin Visitors' Center (p45).

■ This was the second building that Wright designed for his mother's sisters Jane and Nell; the first, Hillside Home School I, was built in 1887. This earlier school was to the east of the present building, in what is now a parking lot. It was constructed in the manner of Joseph Lyman Silsbee, who designed the nearby Unity Chapel, using simple forms and sawn cedar shingles. There were no overhangs, but in the middle of the walls there were two horizontal bands that ran around the school. Behind, to the north, was a boys' dormitory that stood on the site of the drafting room added to this second building in the 1930s.

The second building's south facade was very similar to the Dana House, Springfield, which was to be Wright's next project (see East volume). Interestingly, Susan Lawrence Dana was a benefactor and vice-president of the corporation of Hillside for many years even though she had no children. The stone walls lean slightly inwards at the top, making

the school appear taller than it actually is.

The school was altered after a second-floor fire which was apparently the result of leaf burning. Wright was the only person on the side of the building where the fire began, and John Howe said that he remained quite calm, commenting that he never liked the building's proportions anyway.

The school was successful for many years, but was in financial difficulties by 1915 when Wright purchased it from his aunts for one dollar and converted it into a school for architecture and the allied arts.

Remodeled by the first Taliesin apprentices in 1933, the gymnasium became the theater and the chemistry rooms are now an exhibition space. The apprentices constructed the extension to the north that is now used as a drafting room. Henry-Russell Hitchcock referred to this as an 'abstract forest' due to the density of the open trusses, constructed from timber felled and sawn into rough lumber by the apprentices. Along each side of this room were two rows of bedrooms for the apprentices. The roof and trusses were removed and rebuilt in the 1970s, opening the saw-tooth clerestories, during the early stages of the multi-million dollar restoration program now administered by the Taliesin Preservation Commission. The nearly constant reworking of the school since 1902 has meant that renovation is proving very complicated.

The Midway Barns

The Midway Barns got their name from their location – midway between Taliesin and Hillside. The original structures were left over from one of Wright's uncle's earlier farms. The barns housed a machine shop and dairy for the self-sufficient fellowship. Work was done on the buildings in 1938 and 1947, and they are now to be restored.

ANDREW T PORTER HOUSE,
(Tan-y-Deri)
Spring Green, Wisconsin 53588
1907   0709

TO SPRING
GREEN

23

WISCONSIN RIVER

COUNTY C

COUNTY C

Visitors' Center

PARKING

WELSH HILLS

Porter House ■

JONES VALLEY

23

HILLSIDE RD

Directions: Just north of the Romeo and Juliet Windmill on the Taliesin property.

Accessibility: Tours are occasionally conducted from the Visitors' Center (p45).

■ This basic foursquare design is similar to the Hunt House (see MetroChicago volume) and most of Walter Burley Griffin's work. It is now part of the Taliesin Complex. Mr Porter was Wright's brother-in-law and had previously bought the Heurtley House in Oak Park (see p98 and MetroChicago volume). He moved to Taliesin in 1907 and commissioned this house, becoming an administrator of the Taliesin estate during its early years. This house preceded Taliesin and was built on four acres of John Lloyd Jones' farm, Wright's uncle.

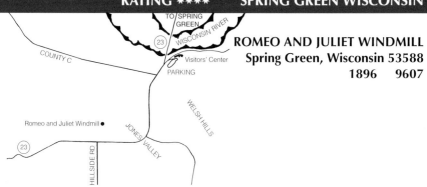

ROMEO AND JULIET WINDMILL
Spring Green, Wisconsin 53588
1896   9607

Directions: On the top of the hill directly north of Hillside Home School.

Accessibility: The windmill is visible from several vantage points and tours are occasionally conducted from the Visitors' Center (p45).

■ Described by Henry-Russell Hitchcock as the marriage of engineering and architecture, this windmill was commissioned by Wright's aunts despite objections from his uncles, who claimed that it would not last the first storm. Ironically, it has remained standing in its original form for nearly a hundred years, a fact that is generally attributed to the bracing floors inside, and the membrane skin outside. Combining the geometries of a lozenge and an octagon, this design incorporates not only a windmill but also a watertower. It was the first restoration project undertaken by the Taliesin Preservation Commission.

UNITY CHAPEL
Cemetery Road
Spring Green, Wisconsin 53588
1886   8601

[Map showing: TO/SPRING GREEN, WISCONSIN RIVER, COUNTY C, 23, Visitors' Center, PARKING, WELSH HILLS, JONES VALLEY, HILLSIDE RD, Unity Chapel, Cemetery]

Directions: East of Hillside Home School in the family cemetery.

Accessibility: The chapel is open occasionally for services and during the annual Lloyd Jones family reunion. More information is available from the Visitors' Center (p45).

■ The architect credited with this family chapel is Joseph Lyman Silsbee who was a friend of Jenkin Lloyd Jones, Wright's uncle and a prominent Unitarian Minister for the south side of Chicago. This was the first time that Wright worked under an architect, and it is not certain exactly what his duties were. He did, however, get a taste for the process. The chapel is set in the family cemetery, concealed within a group of trees, where Mamah Borthwick and many of Wright's relatives are buried, along with many important associates from his apprentice program and architectural practice.

WYOMING VALLEY GRAMMAR SCHOOL
Route 23
Spring Green, Wisconsin 53588
1957   5741

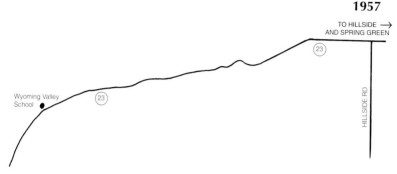

Directions: Located on Route 23, the school is 2 miles past Hillside Home School (pp46-47), after the road curves south, on the west side of the road. It is between Hillside and the House-on-the-Rock.

Accessibility: Visible from Route 23. Unfortunately the building is currently undergoing a change of ownership and accurate information is unavailable. However, it is assumed that access to the property will be possible.

■ This school is very small, approximately 3,000 square feet, and contains only two classrooms and an assembly hall that includes two auxiliary rooms. Like so many of Wright's public buildings, the main entrance is at the center of the composition.

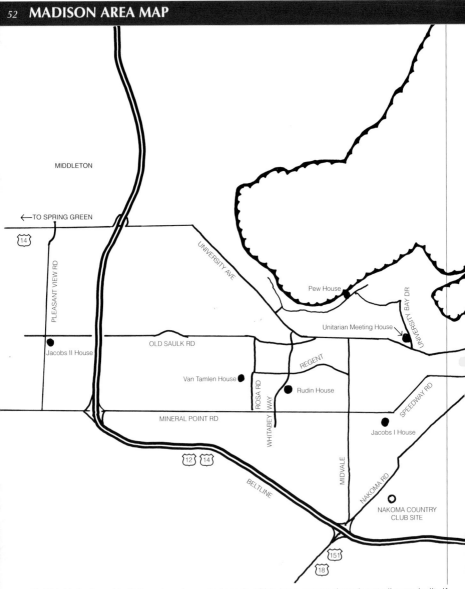

MIDDLETON

←TO SPRING GREEN

(14)

PLEASANT VIEW RD

UNIVERSITY AVE

Pew House

UNIVERSITY BAY DR

OLD SAULK RD

Unitarian Meeting House

Jacobs II House

REGENT

Van Tamlen House

ROSA RD

Rudin House

WHITABEY WAY

SPEEDWAY RD

MINERAL POINT RD

Jacobs I House

(12) (14)

MIDVALE

BELTLINE

NAKOMA RD

NAKOMA COUNTRY
CLUB SITE

(151)

(18)

■ Wright designed buildings here in each decade of his long career, though not all were built. If one had to find a city that summarized Wright's career, this would be it. Madison is where Wright grew up. He met his boyhood friend Robie Lamp here and explored the Madison landscape with him, becoming familiar with many of the future sites of his designs. His home was located on the isthmus a few blocks north of the Lamp House and south of the site for the Yahara Boathouse. He studied civil engineering at the University of Wisconsin and worked for one of his professors on campus. One of his earliest designs was built here and it must have made him and his family proud when he won the competition for the Mendota Boathouse after he had set up his Chicago practice.

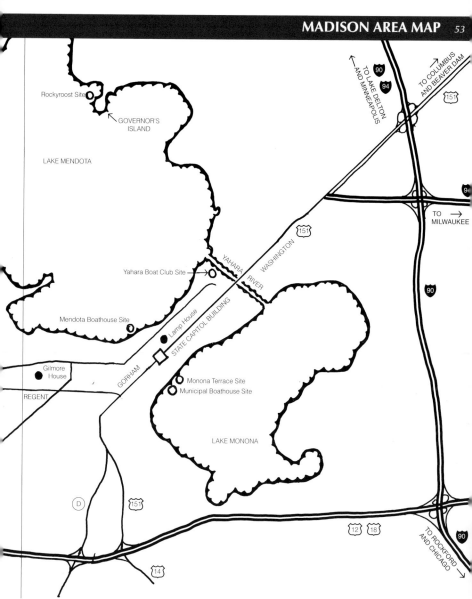

There was a project that was executed in the mid-1920s for the Island Woolen Company of Baraboo, Wisconsin, north of Madison near Lake Delton. William H McFetridge, one of the owners, wrote to Wright concerning the work which involved a dam and observation platforms on the Wisconsin River. It was discovered in 1988 and was published more recently by William A Storrer. There are photographs of it that are dated 1905 and 1913, though the letters to Wright are dated 1924 and 1926. Material on this building can be found at the Saulk County Historical Society and the State Historical Society of Wisconsin. It is located in west Baraboo between 2nd and 8th streets at Ochsner Park. There is little remaining, only one concrete pole.

HERBERT JACOBS II HOUSE
(Solar Hemicycle)
Old Saulk Road
Middleton, Wisconsin 53562
1948   4812

Directions: Located on Old Saulk Road, just east of the church on the corner of Pleasant View Road. The site is southwest of Highway 14 and County C, and west of Madison and Route 12/14 – known as 'The Beltline'. There is no direct exit off Highway 12/14 onto Old Saulk Road.

Accessibility: Only the top few feet of the clerestory and the berm are visible from the road.

■ Known as the Solar Hemicycle, this is the third design by Wright for Herbert Jacobs and the second to be executed. The house was built by the family with some help from

local workmen. The masonry is particularly outstanding. The entrance is through a tunnel into the south-facing sunken garden.

The entire southern elevation is glazed to maximize the warmth of the winter sun, while the overhang of the roof shields the interior during the summer. Like many of Wright's Usonian designs, this house utilizes the thermodynamics of hot and cold air to moderate the internal environment. Hot air rises and cold air falls, a simple concept which is often forgotten in our era of fans and blowers. With Wright's intelligent use of variable ceiling heights and high bands of openable windows, the buildings are very comfortable without requiring chilled and hot air to be blown through a bulky duct system. Indeed, this building incorporates a number of innovative energy-saving ideas – the earth berm to the north, dark energy absorbing floors, and a light, well-insulated roof, as well as those features already mentioned – all of which remain largely neglected in the vast majority of contemporary housing, despite our increased awareness of environmental issues.

The glazed southern wall establishes a visual link between the interior and exterior that is crystallized by the swimming pool which physically connects the two. Mr Jacobs tells how, after a hard day on the farm, he would use this as a plunge pool to cool off on hot summer afternoons.

Entry to the house is unique. One enters the protected, sunken south yard through a tunnel in the earth berm. Any one of the six doors of this elevation can be entered as the inside space is continuous throughout the lower level. Usually the door to the far east is favored. In order to keep the lower level open, the bedrooms on the upper level are hung from the roof with metal rods, the roof joists are supported by the north wall and glazed south wall. This suspension system was also used on the bay/clerestory areas in the Little House living room (p137 and see East volume).

HERBERT JACOBS I HOUSE
441 Toepfer Street
Madison, Wisconsin 53711
1936   3702

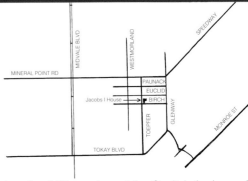

Directions: Southwest of the University of Wisconsin and the Capitol, the house is located one block west and two blocks south of the intersection of Mineral Point Road and Speedway.

(About a mile directly south of the Jacobs I House is the Nakoma Country Club.)

Accessibility: Front elevation visible from the street.

■ Despite the construction of the Wiley House (p23) a number of years earlier, this building is considered by many people to be the first Usonian House. It is certainly the first design that separated the bedrooms from the living areas in a separate wing, and utilized a planning grid incised into the concrete floor. There is a popular story that the apprentices appropriated culled bricks from the Johnson Wax Building for use in this residence, enabling it to be constructed for less than $5,500. If true, it would seem that Wright was either very particular with the former, or very generous to the latter. Mr Jacobs was a newspaper reporter who wrote a biography on Wright, and his daughter Susan became a lifelong apprentice at Taliesin. Today, the house has been lovingly restored by its current owner.

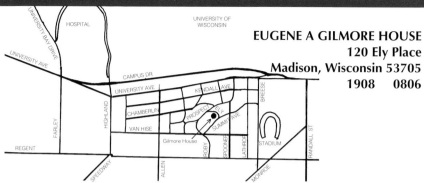

EUGENE A GILMORE HOUSE
120 Ely Place
Madison, Wisconsin 53705
1908   0806

Directions: The house is just west of the university, south of University Avenue, between Roby and Summit streets. Take Roby south from University Avenue for two blocks to Ely Place.

(This house is in a neighborhood of architectural gems: just to the right of this residence is one designed by George Maher, and two blocks to the west, on Prospect Street, is Louis Sullivan's Bradley House – occasionally open to individual visitation if one asks politely.)

Accessibility: Exterior visible to the public.

■ This house is built on an impressive site on the top of a hill. Wright's interior has been retained, including the early kitchen appliances, although some of the furniture was donated to a university. Gilmore was an attorney who taught at the University of Wisconsin and was appointed Vice-Governor of the Philippines by President Harding in 1922. He commissioned Wright to 'create an attractive home with an artistic design' and supervised the construction himself. Strangely the family occupied the house only until the autumn of 1908. At some point before 1942 it was used as a fraternity house. It is now a private residence.

NAUTICAL BUILDINGS

Madison was the site of many nautical buildings designed by Wright. Some of these were built and later demolished, some were never built, and another is now being constructed from a design made in the 1950s.

Mendota Boathouse, Langdon and Carroll Streets
1893   9304

■ Destroyed in February 1926, this boathouse stood on the southeast shore of Lake Mendota by the university near Langdon and Carroll streets. The building formed a 'U' plan, and was set between two shingled towers in what is now known as Olin Park. The site can be located on the north side of west Carroll Street.

Rockyroost (Robert M Lamp Cottage)
1893   9301

■ Rockyroost is now destroyed, as is the island on the north side of Lake Mendota where it once stood. John O Holzhueter's article in the Winter 1988 *Wisconsin Magazine of History* gives the full story of this building and many insights into other projects for Robert Lamp. The site is just northwest of Governor's Island which is accessible only through the grounds of the State Mental Hospital.

Municipal Boathouse, Lake Monona
1893   9308

■ This boathouse was to be considerably larger than the Mendota example. Its roof was engineered with inverted trusses in much the same way as Allan Connover's Radio Hall at the University of Wisconsin. The intended location was the current Monona Terrace site.

Yahara Boat Club, at the south bank of Yahara River
1905   0211

■ This boathouse was designed for the south shore of the Yahara River which joins the Monona and Mendota lakes, on the isthmus, just north of the Capitol. The plain, simple wall surfaces are reminiscent of those at Unity Temple (see MetroChicago volume). John O Holzhueter wrote an in-depth article about the project in the *Wisconsin Magazine of History*, Spring 1989, demonstrating the level of research that should be made into the background of all Wright buildings, both built and unbuilt.

Monona Terrace, East Martin Luther King Boulevard
1938   3909   (revised 1956-95   5632)

■ A new convention center, based on an interpretation of one of Wright's 1950s designs, is currently being constructed on this site, southeast of the State Capitol on the shore of Lake Monona. The building may be open as early as 1997. Information on visits is not yet available.

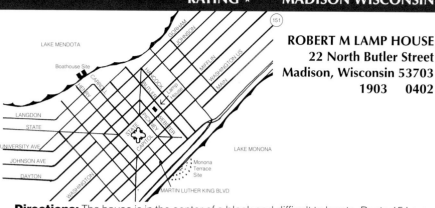

ROBERT M LAMP HOUSE
22 North Butler Street
Madison, Wisconsin 53703
1903   0402

Directions: The house is in the center of a block and difficult to locate. Route 151 runs directly through the center of Madison, and North Butler Street is two blocks north of the State Capitol building.

(Four blocks north, and parallel to Route 151, is Gorham Street, where Wright and Lamp lived when they were children.)

Accessibility: Visible from the drive between the neighboring properties.

■ A very unusual house, especially considering Wright's other work during this period, probably due to the requests of Robert Lamp, a close boyhood friend. The third floor was enclosed, and the brick painted, as early as 1903. This is the earliest flat roofed building Wright designed. Wright was also involved with the design of a lakeside cottage owned by Lamp, on Rockyroost, a small island near Governor's Island, where, as a local newspaper recorded, he stayed with his wife and Edwin and Mamah Cheney (p58). Both the building and the island are now gone.

EUGENE VAN TAMLEN HOUSE
5817 Anchorage Road
Madison, Wisconsin 53705
1956   5518

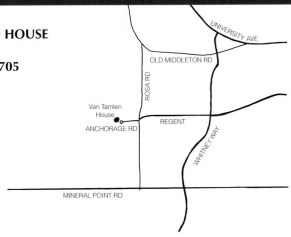

Directions: This house is located in Madison's west side, in an area developed contemporaneously with it. North of Mineral Point Road, and west of Rosa Road, Anchorage Road is the western extension of Regent Street. Anchorage Road is just south of Regent at Rosa Road.

Accessibility: Visible from the street and front drive, although the garden is unfortunately overgrown reducing the view.

■ This is another of the Erdman Prefabs located at the end of a cul-de-sac. It was featured in an article in *House & Home* magazine in December 1956, which showed interior views of the house, including the original color scheme, as well as providing information about the planning of the elevations.

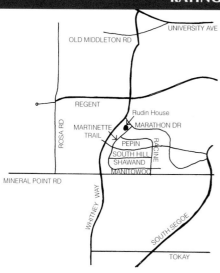

WALTER RUDIN HOUSE
110 Martinette Trail
Madison, Wisconsin 53705
1957   5706

Directions: One block east of Whitney Way, and two blocks north of Mineral Point Road, the house is located at the intersection of Martinette Trail and Marathon Drive, second from the corner, on the west side of the street. It is north of South Hill Drive.

Accessibility: Visible from street. View slightly restricted by foliage.

■ Despite being one of the Erdman Prefabs, this compact square has little to do with the brilliant plan of the Hunt House designed during the Prairie years (see MetroChicago volume). Since the house was built, new structures have been constructed that have restricted the site.

UNITARIAN MEETING HOUSE
900 University Bay Drive
Shorewood Hills, Wisconsin 53705
1947   5031

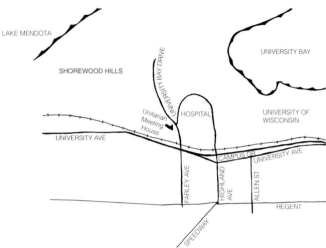

LAKE MENDOTA

SHOREWOOD HILLS

UNIVERSITY BAY

UNIVERSITY BAY DRIVE

Unitarian Meeting House

HOSPITAL

UNIVERSITY OF WISCONSIN

UNIVERSITY AVE

CAMPUS DR
UNIVERSITY AVE

FARLEY AVE

HIGHLAND AVE

ALLEN ST

REGENT

SPEEDWAY

Directions: Shorewood Hills is on the southwest shore of Lake Mendota, adjacent to Madison, and west of the university campus. Take University Avenue about 1.5 miles, turning north onto University Bay Drive/Farley Avenue and continue over the railroad tracks about one block. The church is located on the west side of the street one block after the railroad.

Accessibility: Services are still held in the church, and tours are provided from May to September: Monday to Friday 10am-4pm; Saturday 9am-12pm. Other arrangements may be made by contacting the church on 608-233-9774, or by mail, at least six weeks beforehand.

■ The concept for this church, demonstrated by Wright in his famous television interview with Hugh Downs, is based on a pair of hands folded in prayer and was intended to be the 'church of tomorrow'. The four-acre site was purchased for $21,000 and the contractor for the building was Marshall Erdman, a University of Illinois architecture graduate and novice contractor, who lost over $30,000 on the project due to his inexperience. Mr Erdman idolized Wright and was responsible for the construction of the Erdman Prefabs (pp20, 27, 34, 60, 61, 67, 77).

The building is set on a shallow-pitched gravel bed, similar to the ballast used on railroad tracks, with the walls resting on a mortar skim. The ochre stonework, quarried in nearby Saulk City, has a high quality of finish and workmanship, and complements the green copper roof. The treatment of the glass prow illustrates both Wright's attention to detail and sense of economy. The church was built by Taliesin apprentices, with the assistance of volunteers to save money. Since it was completed there have been two extensions, both of which were designed by Taliesin Associated Architects.

Wright gave the first sermon at the church, and ensured that one of his red square signature tiles was installed in the entrance. The church was founded in 1879 and one of its earliest buildings was designed by the distinguished Boston firm of Peabody and Stearns. Later buildings were designed by Claude and Stark, a local firm of architects, who produced some exceptional Prairie-style designs around Madison.

JOHN C PEW HOUSE
3650 Lake Mendota Drive
Shorewood Hills, Wisconsin 53705
1940   4012

Directions: The house is between the lake and the drive. Lake Mendota Drive runs parallel to the lake and is accessible from either end of University Avenue. The house is on the north side of the street, east of Blackhawk Country Club.

Accessibility: A small part of the rear of the house is visible from the street. The entire facade can be seen from the lake.

■ This a modest sized house that appears monumental due to its position and the projection of the balcony. The house is set diagonally on the site to take advantage of the excellent view of the lake. It is one of the few Usonian Houses that has a second story. A row of doors allows the balcony to become an extension of the living room, while complete privacy is provided by the height of the balcony. Mr Pew was a research chemist for the Forest Products Laboratory in Madison.

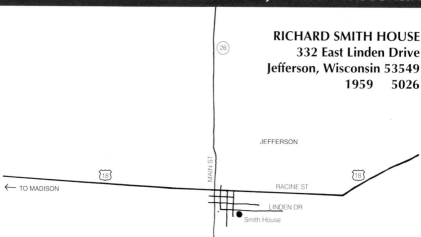

RICHARD SMITH HOUSE
332 East Linden Drive
Jefferson, Wisconsin 53549
1959   5026

Directions: Jefferson is about 32 miles east of Madison on Highway 18, and 6 miles south of Interstate 94, mile 267. Route 26 crosses Interstate 94 and passes through Jefferson, and is named Main Street. Linden is the third street south of Racine Street (Highway 18). The house is three blocks east of Main Street (Route 26) on the south side of the drive.

Accessibility: Partially visible from street.

■ The Smith House has some of the best stonework found in any of Wright's buildings, and, unfortunately, little else of the house is visible. The cantilevered roof gable is an example of the minor engineering marvels that exist in most of Wright's designs, but are often overlooked. The house is all on one level.

E CLARKE ARNOLD HOUSE
954 Dix Street
Columbus, Wisconsin 53925
1954   5401

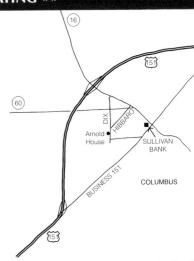

Directions: About 30 miles northeast of Madison, exit Highway 151 east continuing for one block before turning south on to Dix Street. The house is on the west side of the street. (There is a very good Louis Sullivan bank in downtown Columbus which includes some of his best terracotta work and should not be missed.)

Accessibility: Visible from street.

■ Wonderful soft limestone was used in the walls of this house. The front of the house has small windows along the top of the wall, while the rear elevation is more open. There has been a subsequent extension by John H Howe who was a former chief draftsman at Taliesin.

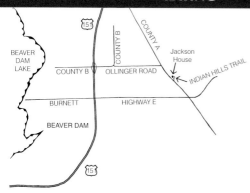

ARNOLD JACKSON HOUSE
7655 Indian Hills Trail
Beaver Dam, Wisconsin 53916
1957   5518

Directions: Beaver Dam is northeast of Madison and Columbus on Highway 151. The house is in a newer subdivision east of County A, between County B (Ollinger Road) to the north and County E (Burnett Road) to the south, to the extreme west of the town, actually out with the farms.

Accessibility: Visible from all sides.

■ This Erdman Prefab has led a nomadic life. It was originally constructed on the Beltline Highway in southwest Madison but, in 1985, it was dismantled and moved to Beaver Dam. Unfortunately, this course of action caused the new owner numerous difficulties and it was only completed with the help of several local residents. The original client, Dr Jackson, was Wright's personal physician in the early 1950s.

These events, as well as the fact that similar houses have different orientations, imply that the positioning of the Erdman Prefabs was not as site specific as Wright's other designs. The main requirement seems to have been a sloping site and a view.

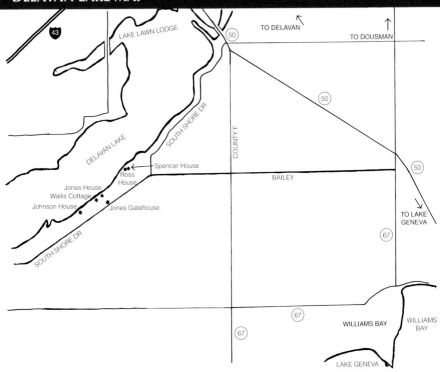

■ The communities of Delavan and Lake Geneva developed as a result of a train connection from Chicago with stops in the western suburbs of Oak Park and River Forest all the way up to Walworth, Wisconsin, a town between Delavan and Lake Geneva. Many of these summer commuters were friends, neighbors and clients of Wright. Usually their first trips brought them to the local hotels and led to some of them purchasing property on the lakes for their own summer homes. These commuters include Wallis and Jones who were responsible for two of the Wright designed houses on South Shore Drive and for raising the money for the Delavan Lake Yacht Club (Opus# 0217). It was built in 1904 on the south shore of Delavan Lake at what is now known as Del Mar Beach. It was moved after the adjacent Golf Club and Yacht Club consolidated. It had been put up for sale but there were no takers. After deciding that it did not fit at its new site, it was torn down in 1916. (Wendy Luttrell wrote a book on the history of the Yacht Club that includes a discussion of this building.)

In the town of Lake Geneva, to the south and east of Delavan Lake, the Lake Geneva Hotel was built in 1912 (Opus# 1202). This long, stucco building once dominated the town's lakefront. It was commissioned by Arthur Richards and his partner. The Lake Geneva Hotel was demolished in 1970 with little protest. Richards was also responsible for the American Systems Buildings (p79) in Milwaukee and elsewhere.

GEORGE W SPENCER HOUSE
3209 South Shore Drive
Delavan, Wisconsin 53115
1902   0207

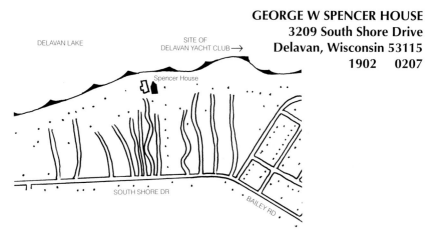

Directions: West on South Shore Drive, it shares a driveway with the Ross House to the west (see map p68).

Accessibility: Visible from the lake but not from the road.

■ This is a simple summer cottage which is distinguished only by its boat-like prow that faces the lake. The house is crammed between two others near the shore.

Photo showing the George W Spencer House (left) and the Charles S Ross House (right)

CHARLES S ROSS HOUSE
**3211 South Shore Drive
Delavan, Wisconsin 53115
1902   0206**

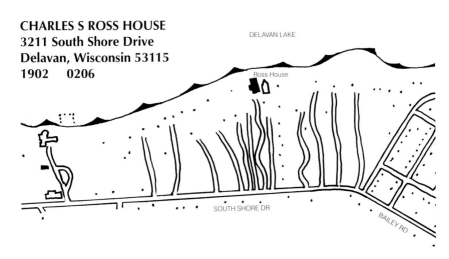

Directions: The north side of South Shore Drive, five drives past the Bailey Road turn (see map p68).

Accessibility: Visible from the lake only.

■ The Ross House is a very innovative building that has been obscured by subsequent extensions. It would be fairly simple to restore this house, but not without dramatically reducing the current floor area. The original design had horizontal board and batten cladding which identified it with Wright's Forest Houses. In the 1940s, Henry-Russell Hitchcock included this house in his short list of outstanding Wright buildings.

FRED B JONES GATEHOUSE
3335 South Shore Drive
Delavan, Wisconsin 53115
1900   0103

GPS: N 42 35.598
        W 88 36.641

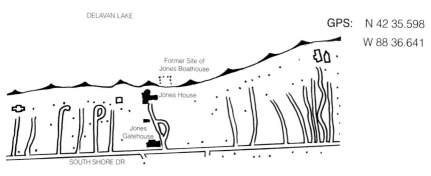

DELAVAN LAKE

Former Site of
Jones Boathouse

Jones House

Jones
Gatehouse

SOUTH SHORE DR

Directions: West on South Shore Drive (see map p68).

Accessibility: Visible from the road.

■ This property originally incorporated several buildings, including a boathouse that burnt down, which the present owners are considering rebuilding. Very little is known about Fred Jones or his involvement with the design process. The tower was originally used for water storage and included a greenhouse. The construction of the dormer windows is similar to those of the Foster House (see MetroChicago volume). The gatehouse is now separately owned.

FRED B JONES HOUSE
3335 South Shore Drive
Delavan, Wisconsin 53115
1900   0103

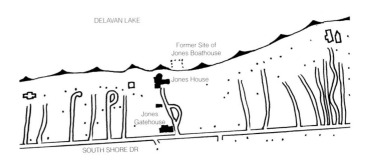

DELAVAN LAKE

Former Site of
Jones Boathouse

Jones House

Jones
Gatehouse

SOUTH SHORE DR

Directions: West on South Shore Drive (see map p68).

Accessibility: Only visible from the lake. The grounds are private and the house is currently undergoing extensive restoration.

■ The architectural features of this residence are unusual for Wright's work during this period, but are similar to those he had produced previously. It is possible, although there is no evidence to suggest this, that the house was designed four or five years earlier and that there was a substantial delay before work commenced on site.

HENRY WALLIS COTTAGE
3407 South Shore Drive
Delavan, Wisconsin 53115
1900   0114

GPS: N 42 35.571
W 88 36.820

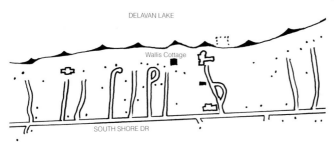

DELAVAN LAKE

Wallis Cottage

SOUTH SHORE DR

Directions: West on South Shore Drive (see map p68).

Accessibility: Visible from both road and lake, though view is partially obstructed by vegetation. The least elaborate facade faces the lake.

■ Despite being a rather modest design, the plan of this house is similar to the much more elaborate Ward Willits House (see MetroChicago volume). The simple geometry of the scheme is expressed clearly throughout. The wooden bands are not just decorative but are positioned to accommodate the expansion and contraction of the stucco. Wallis never lived in the house and it was sold to Dr H Goodsmith upon completion.

AP JOHNSON HOUSE
3455 South Shore Drive
Delavan, Wisconsin 53115
1905   0508

GPS: N 42 35.363
      W 88 36.956

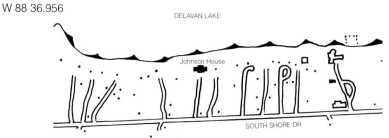

Directions: West on South Shore Drive (p68).

Accessibility: Visible from both the road and the shore.

■ This is one of the few symmetrical houses designed by Wright. Since its construction the porches have been weatherproofed and the interior has many modern improvements. The entire house has a new concrete foundation – including a small basement – which, despite being very expensive, will help to ensure the structure's longevity. The two-story garage to the right was designed by the owners in the 1990s. This site, with its rather high bluff, has a magnificent view of the lake.

COUNTY D

↑ TO DOUSMAN

67

COUNTY D

Greenberg
House

COUNTY C

67

TO DELAVAN

MAURICE GREENBERG HOUSE
3902 Highway 67
Dousman, Wisconsin 53118
1954   5409

GPS: N 42 58.420
W 88 28.224

Directions: On Route 67. Coming from the north, the house is 7 miles south of Interstate 94, 3 miles south of Dousman, and 0.8 miles south of the intersection of County D. Coming from the south, it is 1.4 miles north of the intersection of County C. Route 67 continues south to Delavan another 30 miles.
(Just north of Interstate 94, and a few miles further west, is Ixonia where Wright's family first settled after emigrating from Wales in 1844. A number of his ancestors are buried there.)

Accessibility: Not visible. Beware of the dogs.

■ Although the walls were begun in stone, they had to be torn down after the available supply ran out and the house was constructed from brick. The cantilevers of this house are very similar to those of Fallingwater (see East volume). The spaces inside are unusual for Wright, but not altogether unfamiliar. Due to financial restraints the bedroom wing was never completed even though the bricks for it remain on site.

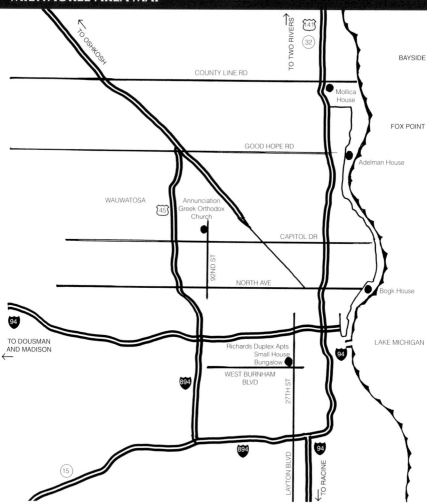

TO OSHKOSH

TO TWO RIVERS

141

32

BAYSIDE

COUNTY LINE RD

Mollica House

FOX POINT

GOOD HOPE RD

Adelman House

WAUWATOSA

45

Annunciation Greek Orthodox Church

CAPITOL DR

92ND ST

NORTH AVE

Bogk House

94

TO DOUSMAN AND MADISON

Richards Duplex Apts Small House Bungalow

LAKE MICHIGAN

94

894

WEST BURNHAM BLVD

27TH ST

15

894

LAYTON BLVD

94

TO RACINE

■ Miriam Noel wrote a letter of condolence to Wright after the Taliesin tragedy, and he was so taken by it that the two of them met soon after. They immediately struck up a tumultuous relationship that continued into the 1920s. Wright divorced his first wife Catherine and married Miriam a year later in 1923. Miriam divorced Wright in August 1928 and died in Milwaukee in 1930. Her grave can be found in the Forest Home Cemetery, but there are no family members buried nearby. The cemetery is just south of downtown, to the east of the American Systems Buildings.

The mural at the Dana House (see East volume) was painted by George Niedecken who went on to form the firm Niedecken-Wallbridge. This company was located in Milwaukee and produced the furnishings for several Wright buildings including the Bogk House (p85). Their papers, including many drawings, are now located in the Prairie Archives at the Milwaukee Art Museum, located on the lakefront in downtown Milwaukee. Some of their work is on permanent display.

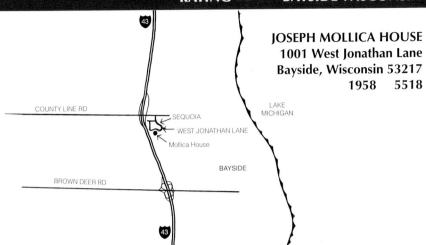

JOSEPH MOLLICA HOUSE
1001 West Jonathan Lane
Bayside, Wisconsin 53217
1958   5518

Directions: Bayside is just north of Fox Point and is accessible off Interstate 43. It is south of the County Line Road separating Milwaukee and Ozaukee, and just east of Interstate 43. Take Sequoia south and turn west on to West Jonathan Lane.

Accessibility: Visible from street.

■ This Erdman Prefab incorporates some of the best stonework in Wisconsin, easily comparable with Taliesin, and is one of a few Wright designs that has an enclosed garage. Despite its age the house appears to have been built in the last few years, but does not stand out in its neighborhood as most of his buildings do. The design of the details and scale of the project are rather simple, although the landscaping is worthy of note.

ALBERT ADELMAN HOUSE
7111 North Barnett
Fox Point, Wisconsin 53217
1948   4801

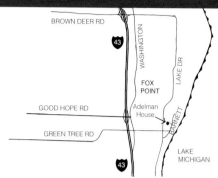

Directions: Fox Point is north of Milwaukee, just north of Whitefish Bay. Exit Interstate 43 at mile 80 east on Good Hope Road. Proceed east to Washington, which is the first intersection east of the exit. Travel south on Washington one block turning east onto Green Tree Road. Continue for just over 0.5 miles until road dead-ends at North Barnett. The house is north of Green Tree on the west side of North Barnett.

Accessibility: The end of the house is visible from the street, but none of the details can be appreciated.

■ This linear house is set well back from the road on a very large suburban lot. The cool gray concrete blocks of the walls contrast with the warm wood of the cabinets and ceiling inside, and the lush landscaping outside. The Adelmans owned a very large laundry and cleaning business that serviced the whole Milwaukee area. The family have lived in the house since it was constructed, which is an increasingly rare occurrence for Wright's buildings. The residence has been retained in its original condition, although some of the period furnishings have been sold.

THE AMERICAN SYSTEMS BUILDINGS
Demonstration Site
Block 2700 West Burnham Boulevard
Milwaukee, Wisconsin 53215
1916   1606

■ The first prototypes for the American Systems Buildings were designed for the Richards Company in 1911. The buildings are not prefabricated, rather the idea was to pre-cut and label each piece of lumber, to transport them to site, and to erect the building according to the accompanying plans. This was intended to be a very efficient system, and was subsequently adopted by other manufacturers including Sears & Roebuck. The archives at Taliesin contain hundreds of drawings for the buildings in this series, and many different types were constructed including one- and two-story houses and duplexes.

Wright would not necessarily have been aware of each individual sale, making it difficult to compile a full inventory from his files – a situation exacerbated by the fact that the original records of the company have not been located, and the archives at Taliesin have few addresses. However, the Milwaukee group of buildings (pp80-82) does give an idea of what a city of Wright designed buildings might have looked like, despite some later alterations. (Other American Systems were built in the MetroChicago area.)

The initial designs were produced in 1911, just after Wright's return from Europe, but the first buildings were not constructed until 1916. The technical drawings were produced by Antonin Raymond and Russell Barr Williamson. The construction of most of these residences was supervised by Williamson, the designer of many other innovative houses in the Milwaukee area, while Raymond drafted most of the presentation drawings.

Three of Arthur Richard's partners – JW Kellogg, Edward Schroeder and E Ebenshade – had houses designed by Wright for Milwaukee, although none were built. A fourth partner, Frederick C Bogk, had a magnificent house built near the lake shore (p85). In 1911 Wright designed a Chinese restaurant in Milwaukee, and hotels at Madison and Lake Geneva for Richards, but only the Lake Geneva Hotel near Lake Delavan was built. Sadly it was demolished in 1970.

Wright broke with the sponsors when the First World War broke out. The American Systems Buildings demonstrate that Wright was not only thinking in terms of mansions for millionaires, but also that he was ahead of most of his contemporaries in facing the problems of mass shelter, as Hitchcock has said.

Examples of this building type are still being identified. As recently as January 1996, one was located in Gary, Indiana. Others have been found in Wilmette and Lake Bluff, Illinois. Unfortunately, at least one major example has already been lost. Destroyed in 1973 to widen the street, the Arthur Munkwitz Apartments could have been moved or the street could have been redesigned to accommodate them. Their loss is tragic and unnecessary. The Munkwitz Apartments were located on 27th Street on the north 100 block, just north of Interstate 94.

RICHARDS DUPLEX APARTMENTS
2720 to 2734 West Burnham Boulevard
Milwaukee, Wisconsin 53215
1916   1605

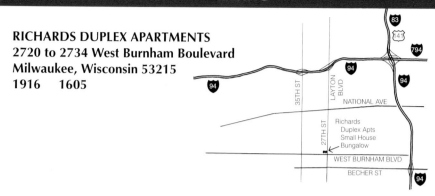

Directions: Exit Interstate 94, west of downtown Milwaukee, at 27th Street/Layton Boulevard and continue south for approximately one mile. Turn west on to West Burnham Boulevard. The apartments are on the north side of the street.

Accessibility: Completely visible from the street.

■ These buildings were ignored for many years and as a result were clad with a variety of discordant materials. They are now being restored. There are two apartments in each of these four buildings; one on each floor. The plan of each unit is identical, except for the western duplex that was flipped to locate the entrance away from the street corner.

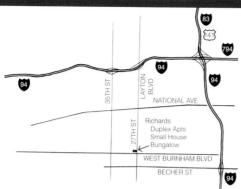

RICHARDS SMALL HOUSE
2714 West Burnham Boulevard
Milwaukee, Wisconsin 53215
1916   1605

Directions: Exit Interstate 94, west of downtown Milwaukee, at 27th Street/Layton Boulevard and continue south for approximately one mile. Turn west on to West Burnham Boulevard. The house is on the north side of the street.

Accessibility: The major facades are visible from street.

■ This is the only known example of this type of small house design. It is easily differentiated from the bungalow by the flat roof, the marginally larger bay window, and the lack of a porch. The area allocated for the kitchen is smaller in the house, although an area was provided for eating.

RICHARDS BUNGALOW
Block 2700, West Burnham Boulevard
Milwaukee, Wisconsin 53215
1916   1605

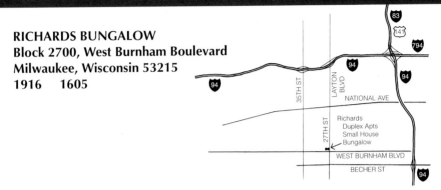

Directions: Exit Interstate 94, west of downtown Milwaukee, at 27th Street, and continue south for approximately one mile. Turn west on to West Burnham Boulevard. The house is on the north side of the street.

(West of Interstate 94 and West Burnham Boulevard are the Milwaukee Botanic Gardens. Just north of Interstate 94, on Block 1100 of 27th Street, was the site of the Munkwitz Apartments which were demolished to accommodate street widening.)

Accessibility: Completely visible from street.

■ To date, this bungalow design was the most widely built of all of the American System units. Examples are to be found here at Milwaukee and in the suburbs of Chicago, about 70 miles to the south. These bungalows are not identical, but are certainly constructed within the same narrow limits. The Hunt Bungalow (p35) is included in this generic group but differs from the Richards Bungalow in that it is on a larger lot that allows a wider overhang for the bedrooms.

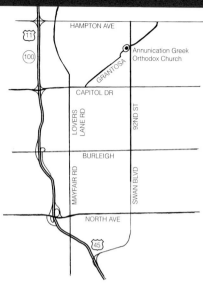

**ANNUNCIATION
GREEK ORTHODOX CHURCH**
9400 West Congress Street
Wauwatosa, Wisconsin 53225
1956   5611

Directions: Northwest of downtown Milwaukee, just east of Highway 45. Exit east on Capitol Drive, and continue for 1.5 miles turning north on to 92nd Street. The church is on the west side of the street, less than 1 mile after the turn.

Accessibility: Visible from the street. Tours are possible if arranged in advance: call 414-461-9400 or write. There is a dress code in order to enter the church.

■ This is a great structure, on an ample site, which won a prestigious award for concrete design. The dome is set on steel balls that allow it to expand and contract without

cracking. The art glass windows were installed many years after the building's completion and were not designed by Wright. Originally the dome was composed of small blue ceramic tiles which have been replaced with synthetic roofing. The plan is a Greek cross, and three spiral staircases, with central light posts, bring people up from the parking to the auditorium. Due to the gently sloping site, the church appears very tall from the west; less so from the east. Many people in the area refer to it as the 'Flying Saucer' for obvious reasons. The interior is breathtaking and appears larger than the exterior. This effect is compounded by the fact that there are no relative points of reference and few elements to assist in the judgement of distance. The ceiling is gold leaf, which intensifies the ambience created by the glazing and lighting. Greek Orthodox iconography has been integrated into the design as required. Wright's wife provided many ideas for the interior design.

Unfortunately, Wright did not live long enough to see the completion of the structure, and, due to financial restraints, a number of the details were simplified or eliminated.

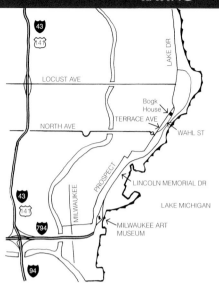

FREDERICK C BOGK HOUSE
2420 Terrace Avenue
Milwaukee, Wisconsin 53211
1916   1602

Directions: About 1 mile north of downtown Milwaukee, one block off the lake and Wahl Street, and two blocks north of North Avenue and St Mary's Hospital. Off Highway 141, take Locust Avenue exit east to the lake, turn south three blocks to Terrace Avenue and one block further. The house is on the east side of the street.

Accessibility: The best facades are visible from the street.

■ The house is an often overlooked masterpiece, perfectly preserved both internally and externally. It effortlessly combines the basic with the sophisticated, the simplicity of

the plan contrasting with the complexity of the elevations.

This plan is based on a very popular and efficient design that appeared originally in the *Ladies Home Journal* in 1907 and which was subsequently constructed in LaGrange, near Chicago, for Stephen Hunt (see MetroChicago volume). Most of the houses designed by Walter Burley Griffin, Wright's protégé, are based on this arrangement. The front half of the building is allocated to the living room, while the rear is divided equally between the dining room and kitchen. Wright usually expressed the entrance and stairway more strongly than here. The Bogk House was the largest and most elaborate of all of the four-square houses and cost $15,000 when it was constructed. The family lived in the house until 1953.

Beneath the eaves is a terracotta frieze depicting human figures with outstretched arms, which is similar to those used at the Imperial Hotel, Tokyo, and the Midway Gardens, Chicago. Nearly all of the original furniture is still in the house and the dining room chairs are particularly notable because of the caning used on the backs. The original carpets and window treatments are preserved in the Prairie Archives at the Milwaukee Art Museum a short distance to the south.

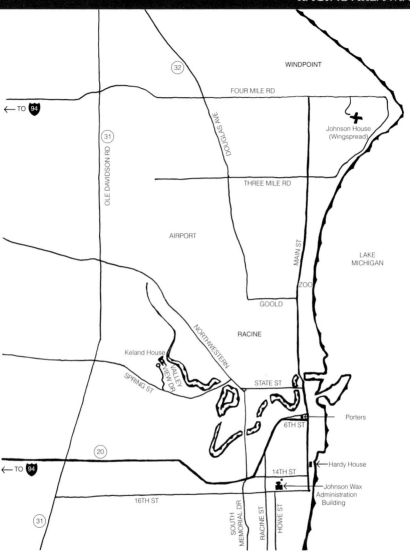

■ Wright's house for Hardy was one of his first outside the Chicago area, though no one has yet discovered how Hardy came to employ the architect. Wright also designed two schemes for the Racine YWCA in 1949 and 1950 (Opus# 4920 and 5041), though neither was built. Racine is more famously the location of three important buildings designed by Wright for the Johnson family – Wingspread, the Keland House and the Johnson Wax Company buildings. The Johnson family have been very generous to the Racine community, and were responsible for commissioning the Prairie School designed by Charles Montooth of Taliesin (which is located just south of Wingspread).

HERBERT F JOHNSON HOUSE, (Wingspread)
33 East 4 Mile Road
Wind Point, Wisconsin 53402
1937   3703

GPS: N 42 47.050
         W 87 46.274

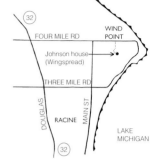

Directions: West of the lake on Four Mile Road, 4 miles north of downtown Racine. From Racine, take Main Street – the street the Hardy House is on – north until it dead-ends at Four Mile Road. From Interstate 94 at mile 329, County K, take the Interstate East Frontage Road approximately 0.5 miles to Four Mile Road. Proceed east approximately 10 miles to the house. The entrance is clearly marked with a sign.

Accessibility: No access to the public. However, the house and grounds are accessible to those participating in the foundation's programs. Members of the public are free to write to them and request information.

■ One of the few large houses for wealthy clients, Wingspread is among Wright's best. The central space, accessed from the low entrance vestibule, is certainly one his finest interiors and acts as a focus for the four wings of the house, each of which contains a separate function.

     The interior is finished in oak rather than the darker American walnut used in the Johnson Wax Administration Building. A seldom seen classical dentil detail is found

throughout the interior, on desks, chairs and tables. The dining table was initially designed to be drawn into the kitchen between courses, but as this proved awkward it was permanently attached to the wall. Smaller units can be attached to the open end to accommodate more people.

According to Sam Johnson, the son of the original client, this table is the site of the famous water leak story. The senior Mr Johnson was holding a dinner party for a number of guests, including the Governor of Wisconsin. Unfortunately, during the course of the meal water began to drip on to his forehead. Enraged, Mr Johnson ordered Sam to bring the telephone to the table and phoned Wright. He angrily explained the situation to the architect and demanded an immediate solution. Wright calmly suggested that he move his chair.

The deep brick fins make the interior appear very open from the inside, and the exterior dark and secluded from the outside. Internally the wings retain many details from the original structure, despite being converted into seminar rooms for the current occupants, The Johnson Foundation. The building, in particular the clerestory of the central pavilion, has recently undergone extensive structural work.

WILLARD H KELAND HOUSE
1425 Valley View Drive
Racine, Wisconsin 53405
1954   5417

GPS: N 42 44.160
       W 87 49.274

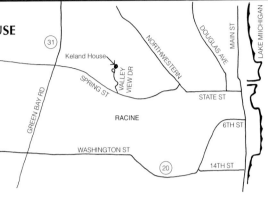

Directions: West and a little north of downtown Racine, 1 mile east of Highway 31 and 1.3 miles west of Highway 38. Valley View Drive goes north from Spring Street. The house is on the east side of the street.

Accessibility: Visible from the street.

■ Wright designed this house for Karen Johnson, daughter of HF Johnson, and her first husband Willard Keland. Keland was responsible for the Riverview Terrace Restaurant (now the Taliesin Visitors' Center at Spring Green (p45)), and was the former President of the Wisconsin River Development Corporation. This is a spatially complex design that has a number of unique features which include the enclosed entrance garden and the two-story living room. The red brick is similar to that used at the Johnson Wax Administration Building.

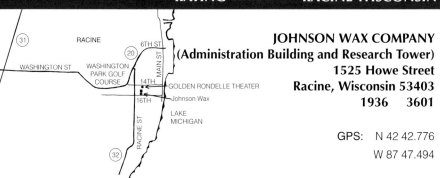

JOHNSON WAX COMPANY
(Administration Building and Research Tower)
1525 Howe Street
Racine, Wisconsin 53403
1936   3601

GPS: N 42 42.776
W 87 47.494

Directions: The main SC Johnson Wax Company campus is south and west of downtown Racine. Exit Interstate 94 at Route 20 and proceed east about 10 miles. Route 20 makes several turns around the Washington Park Golf Course and intersects 14th Street. Proceed east five blocks on 14th to the Golden Rondelle Theater; parking is adjacent. The administration building is on Howe Street.
(The Hardy House is east three blocks to Main Street and north.)

Accessibility: Free public tours are given on a regular basis by reservation only. Contact the Golden Rondelle Theater by writing or calling 414-631-2154. Tours are given Tuesday to Friday at 11.15am and 1pm throughout the year. From March to November, two additional tours are added at 10am and 2.15pm.

■ Wright is best known for his residential work, but the Johnson Wax Building also puts him at the forefront of commercial design. It was certainly a product of its time, with its sleek, streamlined appearance. Unlike other buildings of the period that were often called Art Deco, this building appears moderne without being trendy. It has no plate

glass windows, only Pyrex glass tubes to admit light. At night these become more pronounced, their luminosity making the roof appear to float above the red brick walls. The tubing not only serves to insulate the space, but also to prevent the workers from gazing out of the windows, daydreaming.

When one approaches the Johnson Wax Building, there is an element of surprise as it is smaller than expected. Even the tower cannot be seen from more than a few blocks away, despite appearing very tall in photographs. The building permit was issued on 30 April 1927, building started on 3 September 1936, and work finished on 1 April 1939.

The idea for the mushroom columns was first proposed five years earlier in unexecuted designs for a newspaper building in Salem, Oregon. In the Johnson Wax Building they were a great point of contention. The State building inspectors stopped construction in order to perform a full-scale test to determine their permissible and ultimate carrying weights. The columns were designed to support 12 tons. When tested they were able to hold 60 tons, five times the allowable limit: the inspectors allowed construction to continue.

The interior of the main Administration Building is unexpected. It is like looking through a small grove of concrete trees. The space is very large but the columns create differing effects, at times making it appear larger and at others smaller – one of the visual dichotomies common to many Wright designs. The office furniture is innovative and certainly as moderne as any of the time, yet it also has a timeless quality. The desks have three table levels which could almost have been designed to accommodate today's computer keyboards and screens. Most of the chairs for those working on the main floor were three-legged without wheeled casters, and had pivoted backs. The colours of their original fabric covering included the familiar Cherokee red of the floor and brick, along with a soft blue, green and yellow ochre. The original Cherokee red rubber tiles of the floor are now covered with carpet. The underside of the balcony that surrounds the

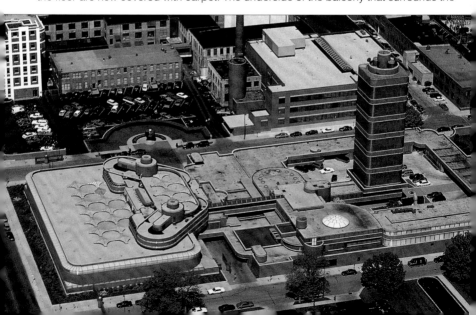

workroom is surfaced with cork to absorb sound. The brass guard rail along the top of the balcony wall was fitted in the early 1970s to conform to OSHA standards, even though no one had fallen from the balcony in the previous thirty-five years. Similar requests to add a metal fire escape to the outside of the tower – which would have destroyed the building's beauty – resulted in its closure.

The Research Tower is a later addition to the Administration Building and was built in the mid 1940s. The walls are not supported from the outside, but by the cantilevered floors that extend from the central spine of the building. This spine also contains all the mechanical systems and the elevator.

The pools and granite sculptures at the base of the Research Tower were added in the late 1970s by Taliesin Associated Architects. The sculptures are upscaled versions of those that were originally designed for the Nakoma Country Club of Madison in the 1920s. Before these additions, the Tower rose directly from the grade level and made a very strong statement.

The Golden Rondelle Theater, where tours of the building begin, was designed by William Wesley Peters, the late chief architect and engineer of Taliesin Associated Architects. Built for the New York World Fair, the Golden Rondelle was flown by helicopter back to Racine.

The Johnson family started business in Racine as a wood flooring company. Responding to inquiries on how to protect these beautiful wooden floors, they decided to produce a protective wax. Through their international travels in search of sources of wax, the Johnsons became advocates of aviation, maintaining several different types of airplane, especially pontoon boats that could land on the rivers in South America. (Johnson outboard motors are not connected with the family, though a separate arm of the company sells the famous Johnson Spoon and other fishing lures.)

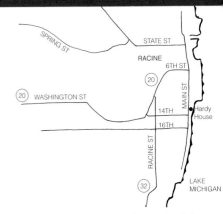

THOMAS P HARDY HOUSE
1319 South Main Street
Racine, Wisconsin 53403
1905   0506

GPS: N 42 42.985
        W 87 46.934

Directions: Main Street is the major north–south street running parallel to the lake. The Hardy House is south of downtown, between 13th and 14th streets.
(There are many other architecturally significant houses on South Main Street, including one attributed to Cecil Corwin. The SC Johnson Wax Company campus (p91) is just a few blocks southwest at 16th and Howe.)

Accessibility: Private with its original high walls. Visible from street, lake and park.

■ This a great house which remains unaltered. The art glass patterns have been removed from the lakeside windows, but can be appreciated from the sidewalk. The symmetry of the east and west facades makes it difficult to determine the front door from the back door. The front door is on the right. There is a famous drawing by Marion Mahoney – a draftswoman in Wright's office – which illustrates the house without the trees that obviously now block the glare from the lake. Mr Hardy was the Mayor of Racine for a time.

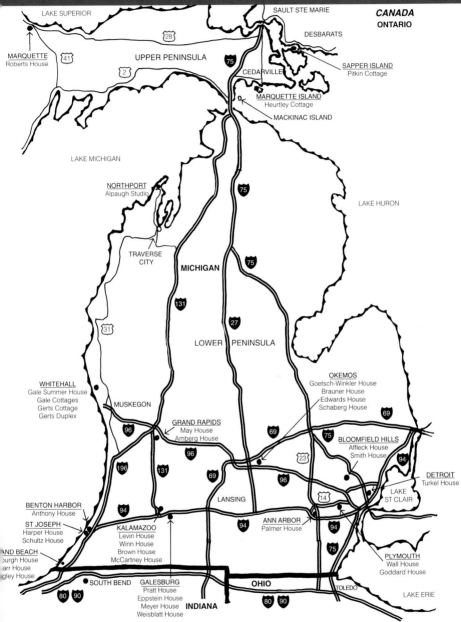

LAKE SUPERIOR

SAULT STE MARIE

CANADA
ONTARIO

DESBARATS

28

UPPER PENINSULA

75

CEDARVILLE

MARQUETTE
Roberts House

41

2

SAPPER ISLAND
Pitkin Cottage

MARQUETTE ISLAND
Heurtley Cottage

MACKINAC ISLAND

LAKE MICHIGAN

NORTHPORT
Alpaugh Studio

75

LAKE HURON

TRAVERSE
CITY

MICHIGAN

131

75

27

LOWER PENINSULA

OKEMOS
Goetsch-Winkler House
Brauner House
Edwards House
Schaberg House

WHITEHALL
Gale Summer House
Gale Cottages
Gerts Cottage
Gerts Duplex

31

MUSKEGON

GRAND RAPIDS
May House
Amberg House

69

BLOOMFIELD HILLS
Affleck House
Smith House

96

96

69

23

75

94

DETROIT
Turkel House

196

131

69

96

LAKE
ST CLAIR

BENTON HARBOR
Anthony House

ST JOSEPH
Harper House
Schultz House

94

LANSING

14

ANN ARBOR
Palmer House

94

94

AND BEACH
ourgh House
arr House
gley House

KALAMAZOO
Levin House
Winn House
Brown House
McCartney House

94

75

PLYMOUTH
Wall House
Goddard House

80 90

SOUTH BEND

GALESBURG
Pratt House
Eppstein House
Meyer House
Weisblatt House

INDIANA

OHIO

80 90

TOLEDO

LAKE ERIE

■ Michigan is the site of two realized multi-family developments, in Galesburg and Kalamazoo, and the proposed site for two additional developments for Detroit and Lansing. Most of the residential sites in Michigan are on sloped sites making the use of balconies and terraces requirements. The Pitkin Summer House in Desbarats, Ontario, is included here because of its proximity to Sault Ste Marie in the Upper Peninsula of Michigan. This is the only remaining building of Wright's design in Canada.

EH PITKIN COTTAGE
Sapper Island
Desbarats, Ontario, Canada
1900   0005

GPS: N 46 18.943
       W 83 57.715

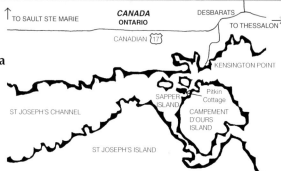

Directions: This house is 28 miles southeast of Sault Ste Marie on an island off Canada Route 17. The house is 0.5 miles to the southwest of Kensington Point, Desbarats, between Picture Island and Campement d'Ours Island, to the north of St Joseph's Island. Sapper Island is so small it can only be found on nautical maps and is only approximately 300 feet wide and 1,000 feet long.

Accessibility: The island is accessible by boat in the summer, and occasionally snowmobile in the winter. If boating, be careful of the very shallow waters that surround the island. The house is to the far west end of the island.

■ This cottage, built for Mr Pitkin, an Oak Park neighbor of Wright, was one of the first residences clad with horizontal siding. There have been few alterations since its construction. The Desbarats area appears to have been a favorite vacation destination for Oak Park residents as Wright designed similar buildings for Victor Metzger (1902) and JA Scudder (1904) on the large island south of Campement d'Ours Island. Neither of these projects was built.

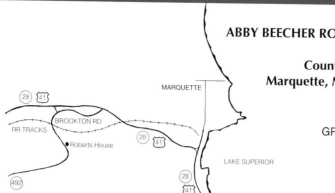

ABBY BEECHER ROBERTS HOUSE,
(Deertrack)
County Highway 492
Marquette, Michigan 49855
1936   3603

GPS: N 46 31.794

W 87 26.585

Directions: West of the city. From Lake Superior take Route 28/41 west for 3 miles. Take the Route 492 exit and continue south for one block onto Brookton Road. Proceed 0.4 miles past the railroad tracks. The house is located before the second curve, on the east side of the road. Brookton Road is behind the commercial strip and the entry is difficult to locate.

Accessibility: The house is in the woods with another structure built against it. Only the living room windows on the east and the entrance portico on the west can be seen.

■ The facades of this house are constructed from an unusual combination of brick and stucco. The client was the mother-in-law of Los Angeles architect John Lautner who built many innovative buildings and was trained at Taliesin during the 1930s. It was completed just before the Jacobs House, Madison (p56), yet cost an astonishing $76,000. Unfortunately, the property has been rented for many years and has fallen into neglect.

ARTHUR HEURTLEY SUMMER COTTAGE
Les Cheneaux Club, Marquette Island
Cedarville, Michigan 49754
1902   0214

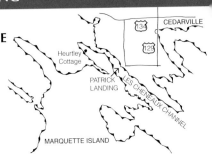

GPS: N 45 59.404
       W 84 23.202

Directions: This site is on an island just south of Cedarville. Cedarville is in Michigan's upper penisula, south and east of the Mackinaw Bridge. Take Interstate 75 east 30 miles to Highway 134. Cedarville is on the shore at Highway 134 and the south end of Highway 129, directly south of Sault Ste Marie. Marquette Island is one of Les Cheneaux Islands, northeast of Mackinac Island in Lake Huron, and is only accessible by boat. The house is on the south shore of the northern most peninsula, the sixth house from the point.

Accessibility: The island can only be reached by boat. All the docks are private. The house is set near the shore but is partially obscured by trees.

■ Arthur Heurtley, a neighbor of Wright's, had the architect work on this cottage while his Oak Park residence (see MetroChicago volume) was being constructed. This design was a remodelling, as noted in 1942 by Henry-Russell Hitchcock in his book *In the Nature of Materials.* The Les Cheneaux Club is a private organization founded by a small group of very wealthy individuals from the Midwest, whose alumni include Henry Ford.

AMY ALPAUGH STUDIO
71 North Peterson Park Road
Northport, Michigan 49670
1947   4703

GPS: N 45 09.116
W 85 38.218

Directions: Northwest of Traverse City, take Route 22 for 26 miles to Northport and 201 (Mill Street). Continue 1 mile north. The building is on a knoll, north of the center of Peterson Park and about 1.2 miles from the end of Mill Street west on Peterson Park Road.

Accessibility: The house is set almost a mile back from the public road, behind several gates and fences, and is extremely difficult to locate. It a still a private home and is not worth pursuing unless invited.

■ This house is positioned at the top of a knoll from where there are views east to Traverse Bay and west to Lake Michigan – probably the most spectacular site of any of Wright's buildings. The interior is tiny and was intended as a studio. Enclosures and alterations have been made since its original construction. It is like the Harper House in St Joseph (p129) with its roof/ceiling facing Lake Michigan. Miss Alpaugh heard Wright give a talk at Cranbrook while she was a student there. After hearing about Mr Jacobs' house (p56), she began with a budget of $7,000, but in the end spent a total of $47,000 on the studio.

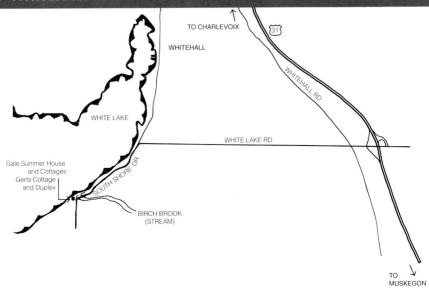

■ North of Whitehall lies the city of Charlevoix, where Wright's River Forest client Edward Waller owned 2,000 acres of land between Lake Michigan and Lake Charlevoix just north of town. Wright designed a number of buildings for this site, but apparently only a bathing pavilion was built (Opus# 0916). It was probably constructed around 1909 and burnt down in the early 1920s. From a photograph published in William Storrer's *Companion,* it appears that the building had a hipped roof and a continuous line of windows. The window pattern appears to be defined by the wooden muntins and is similar to that of the Robie and Ingalls houses of the same time (see MetroChicago volume). There is still a Waller Road in Charlevoix.

In nearby Muskegon, there is a scheme listed for a client named Larwell. There was a Mrs Larwell, a widow, who lived in the town during this period, but her listed address was not a Wright design. It would be interesting to know more about the circumstances of this project.

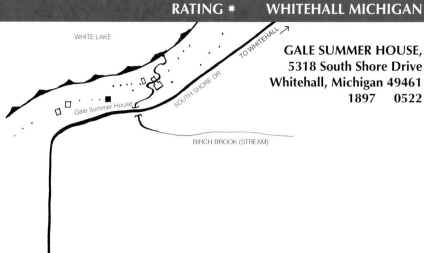

WHITE LAKE

TO WHITEHALL

SOUTH SHORE DR

Gale Summer House

BIRCH BROOK (STREAM)

GALE SUMMER HOUSE,
5318 South Shore Drive
Whitehall, Michigan 49461
1897   0522

Directions: Whitehall is about 45 miles northwest of Grand Rapids, just off the eastern shore of Lake Michigan. Exit Highway 31 at White Lake Road, and head west for 5 miles to South Shore Drive. Proceed southwest for 1 mile and watch for the house numbers.

Accessibility: Visible from the street.

■ This appears to be the first of the buildings built in Whitehall, and seems to have been sited randomly as there are so few features to the landscape. As the value of the land increased it was subdivided and sold off in parcels for development. The building was adjusted to one side in order to keep within the zoning codes, and its original features have been obliterated in subsequent renovations.

GALE COTTAGES
5324 and 5370 South Shore Drive
Whitehall, Michigan 49461
1905   0502

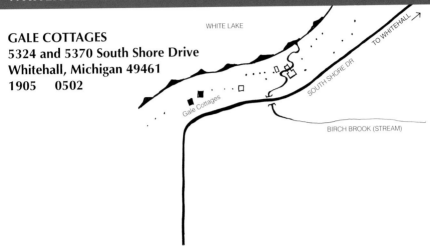

WHITE LAKE

SOUTH SHORE DR

TO WHITEHALL

Gale Cottages

BIRCH BROOK (STREAM)

Directions: There are other buildings on the same site. The exact location can only be identified visually.

Accessibility: As with so many summer vacation homes, they are generally oriented to the outside. Any approach will intrude on the privacy of the occupants.

■ There seem to have been as many as three cottages built for the Gales. It is believed that they were rented out over the summer months rather than having been held for use by other members of the Gale family.

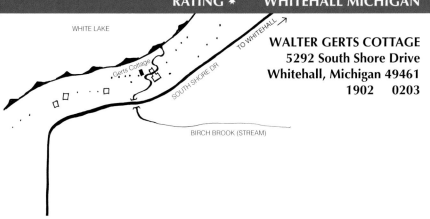

WHITE LAKE

TO WHITEHALL

SOUTH SHORE DR

Gerts Cottage

BIRCH BROOK (STREAM)

WALTER GERTS COTTAGE
5292 South Shore Drive
Whitehall, Michigan 49461
1902   0203

Directions: The house is on the east side of a shared driveway.

Accessibility: The house is below the road and is reached by a driveway on the flat plane just above lake level. With windows on all four sides, it would be disturbing to the occupants to venture close to the house. Little of the original design is visible at any distance.

■ This building started as a wonderfully compact cottage with horizontal board and batten siding. It appears that it was not initially fitted with running water, although it had space for a servant. The building is perfectly designed for a vacation house, with a large open living room and a spacious open porch on the lake side. All this has now changed. The house's orientation was altered when the structure was moved off its foundation, and the open porch is now enclosed with storm windows. Walter Gerts was the son of George Gerts.

GEORGE GERTS DUPLEX
5260 South Shore Drive
Whitehall, Michigan 49461
1902   0202

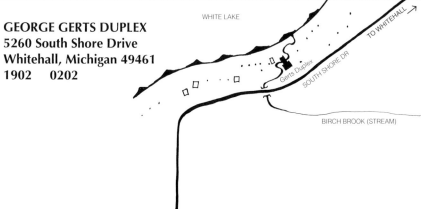

Directions: This house can be located by the street number on South Shore Drive.

Accessibility: One would have to walk past the garage and up to the building in order to see it. With a continuous window band, one cannot avoid disturbing the occupants.

■ The building is set against a steep slope at the back of the house and bridges the stream named Birch Brook. This was a clever solution to a site with a very limited buildable area. The curve of the bridge makes an elegant statement and is on one of the most beautiful lake sites of any Wright-designed house. The duplex has undergone considerable restoration which gives a very good idea of Wright's initial intentions.

The early drawings of this house show it as a single-story building with no bedrooms. As it exists now there is a second floor for the sleeping quarters. George Gerts was a River Forest neighbor of Wright's.

MEYER MAY HOUSE
450 Madison Avenue, SE
Grand Rapids, Michigan 49503
1908   0817

GPS: N 42 57.329

W 85 39.523

Directions: South and a little east of downtown Grand Rapids. Exit Highway 131 at Wealthy Street and proceed east nine blocks to Madison Avenue, then south on Madison for one block. The house is on the east side of the street at the corner.

Accessibility: Free guided tours are given on Tuesday and Thursday from 10am to 1pm, and on Sunday from 1 to 4pm. Reservations are required for tours of more than ten people. Call: 616-246-4821. Tours start at the Visitors' Center.

■ This unusual house, situated just a few hundred yards west of the Amberg House (p106), was perhaps influenced by Marion Mahoney and is well worth a visit. It was in a deteriorated state before the furniture manufacturer Steelcase purchased it in 1987 and restored it to its original condition. Some of the original Niedecken furnishings were found and restored, and reproductions were made when originals were unavailable. Mr May worked in, and later took over, the family's clothing store in Grand Rapids where he invented the swivelling coat rack. The original construction was to have cost $16,000. May persuaded his father-in-law, Mr Amberg, to hire Wright for his house.

JH AMBERG HOUSE
505 College Avenue
Grand Rapids, Michigan 49503
1910   1001

GPS: N 42 57.174
       W 85 39.424

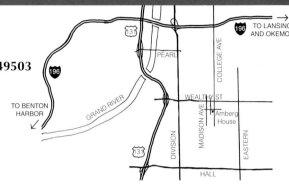

Directions: The house is located on College Avenue in the historic district, eleven blocks east of Highway 131 and two blocks south of Wealthy Street. It is just east of the May House (p105) which is open to the public.

Accessibility: Much can be seen from the street without disturbing the occupants of this private house.

■ The attribution of this house is open to some question. It is obvious that Wright had something to do with its design but little to do with the detailing. In his 1942 book Henry-Russell Hitchcock noted that Wright had done preliminary sketches for the house before his departure for Europe in 1909. He left the commission to Von Holst and Marion Mahoney. Her hand is apparent in the layout and details. Mr Amberg employed Niedecken & Wallbridge to provide the interior furnishings.

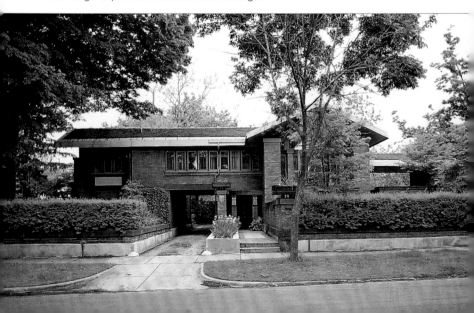

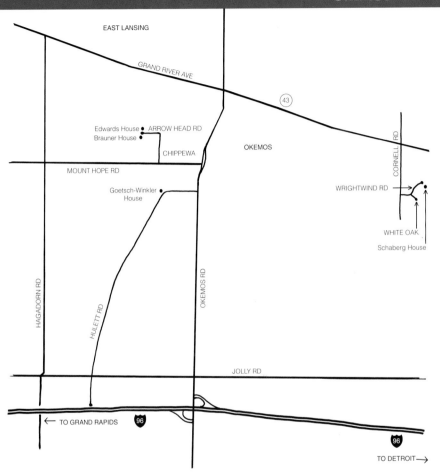

EAST LANSING

GRAND RIVER AVE

43

Edwards House • ARROW HEAD RD
Brauner House •

CHIPPEWA

OKEMOS

CORNELL RD

MOUNT HOPE RD

Goetsch-Winkler •
House

WRIGHTWIND RD →

WHITE OAK

Schaberg House

HAGADORN RD

HULETT RD

OKEMOS RD

JOLLY RD

← TO GRAND RAPIDS   96

96

TO DETROIT→

■ In 1939, Professor Newman of the Michigan State University Psychology Department gathered together a group that included seven faculty professors – Brauner, Garrison, Goetsch, Hause, Panshin, Van Dusen and Winkler – to form a cooperative for housing and a farm collective. Goetsch and Winkler contacted Wright concerning the 40-acre, eight-building project in Lansing, which would have been his first multi-client development of the Usonian period. Wright named it Usonia I (Opus# 3912). Unfortunately, the financing collapsed and subsequent appeals to the Federal Housing Authority, Washington, DC, were rejected. The FHA felt that they would be unable to sell the properties due to their impractical underfloor heating and lack of roof support. The contractor, Harold Turner, was ready to break ground when the scheme was called off.

GOETSCH-WINKLER HOUSE
2410 Hulett Road
Okemos, Michigan 48864
1939   3907

MOUNT HOPE RD

Goetsch-Winkler House

HULETT RD

OKEMOS RD

Directions: Exit Interstate 96 at mile 110. Take Okemos Road north for 2 miles to Hulett Road, then go west to the next corner. Hulett Road is marked in both directions. The house is on the west side of the street, just at the turn.

Accessibility: One cannot walk past the carport without being seen from the windows and doors on the lawn side. There is a view from the south during the winter.

■ This small, quiet house in a wooded, although urban, setting was designed by Wright for two women from the Art Department at the University of Michigan. The kitchen is just inside the carport and is separated from the bedrooms by the combined dining and living room. The wood detailing is excellent and still in very good condition. Walls are redwood and ceilings are fir plywood. One of the earliest of Wright's Usonian Houses, it was to have been one of a group of seven. At 1,350 square feet, it is the same size as the L-shaped Jacobs I House (p56) but is set in a straight line. When Alma Goetsch and Katherine Winkler retired to Arkansas they commissioned E Fay Jones to design their new house.

ERLING BRAUNER HOUSE
2527 Arrow Head Road
Okemos, Michigan 48864
1948   4601

Directions: Exit Interstate 96 at mile 110 (Okemos Road) and travel north for 2.4 miles to Mount Hope Road, then west for 0.7 miles to Chippewa. Go north on Chippewa for one long block to Arrow Head Road. Travel west on Arrow Head to the dead end. The house is on the south side of the circle turn around. The Edwards House (p110) is to the north.

Accessibility: Visible from the street. Do not venture around the back.

■ This wonderful small house sits on a large site with views to the south and west. It has everything. Variations in the site give each side of the house such different characters that they are almost unrecognizable as the same building. The pool and unusual interior were restored by the owner, who is an architect practicing in the area. The built-in seating is not connected to the central fireplace. The tiny bathroom with its skylight and high ceiling is an example of a masterful handling of small spaces. The concrete block can be easily overlooked because it is now painted. The Brauners were part of the original co-operative group, along with Miss Goetsch and Miss Winkler, which had planned the first group housing often called Usonia I.

JAMES EDWARDS HOUSE
2504 Arrow Head Road
Okemos, Michigan 48864
1949   4904

Directions: Exit Interstate 96 at mile 110. Take Okemos Road northwards for 2.4 miles to Mount Hope Road, then west for 0.7 miles to Chippewa. Travel north on Chippewa for one long block until Arrow Head Road. Travel west on Arrow Head to the dead end. The house is on the north side of the circle turn around. The Brauner House is to the south (p109).

Accessibility: Visible from street.

■ The beautiful red-orange brick gives warmth to this compact Usonian House. The Edwards were not connected to the University but were neighbors of the Schabergs who had asked Wright for a design several years earlier. Mr Edwards read an article by Loren Pope in the August 1948 edition of *House Beautiful,* then wrote to Wright on 2 August, 1948. Edwards watched the construction of the Schaberg (p111) and Palmer (p118) houses, visited the Affleck House (p115), and spoke to Alma Goetsch before going ahead with his own project.

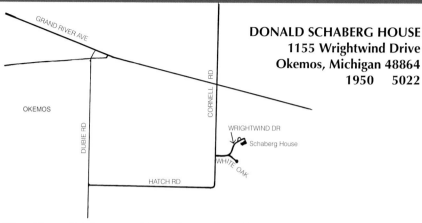

DONALD SCHABERG HOUSE
1155 Wrightwind Drive
Okemos, Michigan 48864
1950   5022

Directions: Exit Interstate 96 at mile 110. Take Okemos Road north through town to Grand River Avenue and then east 2 miles to Cornell Road. Turn south on Cornell and travel 0.4 miles to White Oak (across from Cornell School). Take the north fork on to Wrightwind. The Schaberg House is the last house on the south side of the street.

Accessibility: Very little can be seen without disturbing the occupants.

■ This is a very large house (nearly 4,000 square feet) on a 7-acre site at the far east edge of Okemos. It was designed in 1950 but not built until 1958. It is one of the few houses to retain its original furnishings and one of the very few Wright houses with a swimming pool. The main views of the house are to the southeast, its back and entrance facing northwest. Recently the Taliesin Preservation Committee updated the dining and living room areas. Mr Schaberg owns a very successful lumber business in Lansing.

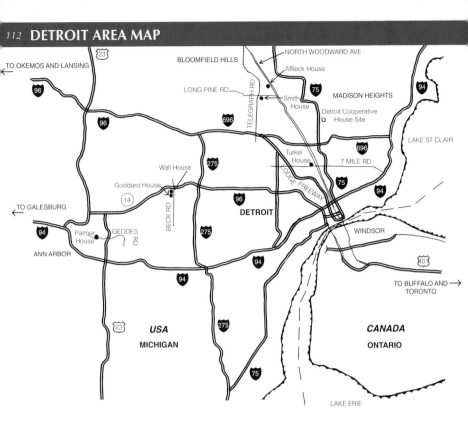

■ Wright's Cooperative Housing (Opus # 4201), located in Madison Heights, east of Royal Oak and just north of Detroit, was intended to house twenty-two families on 120 acres. Each dwelling was to cost $1,600 and be constructed using a method of rammed earth consisting of 70 per cent sand and 30 per cent clay. A prototype was begun in 1940, but abandoned when the US entered the war. Mr Harpers Ferry was one of the strongest proponents of the project. The Circle Pines project for Cedarville (Opus # 4205) was a direct result of Wright's experience with these buildings.

Henry Ford commissioned a large house from Wright, just before the architect's departure for Europe with Mamah Borthwick Cheney in 1909. Ford may have become acquainted with Wright through Arthur Heurtley, of the Northern Trust Bank, Chicago, as they were both members of Les Cheneaux Club that owned property at Cedarville (p98). Unfortunately, Ford became dissatisfied with the design and the handling of the project, and the scheme was abandoned.

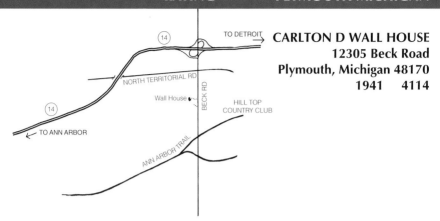

CARLTON D WALL HOUSE
12305 Beck Road
Plymouth, Michigan 48170
1941   4114

Directions: Take Exit 18 off Route 14 at Beck Road. Travel south on Beck Road for 0.7 miles. The House is on the west side of the road.

Accessibility: The house is set well back on the site and cannot be seen from the street. Walking down the drive is not a good idea as it would disturb the occupants.

■ This wonderful house is based on a hexagon, and Wright called it 'Snowflake', in reference to its hexagonal planning grid. The brickwork gives just the right amount of texture to contrast with the smooth roof. Extended walls and terraces remind one of Wright's stated aim: to make one ponder where the garden ends and the building begins. The house was once owned by Thomas Monaghan as a part of his Frank Lloyd Wright Study Center. It was returned to use as a residence in the late 1980s. The Walls met at Olivet College and married in their early twenties.

LEWIS H GODDARD HOUSE
12221 Beck Road
Plymouth, Michigan 48170
1953   5317

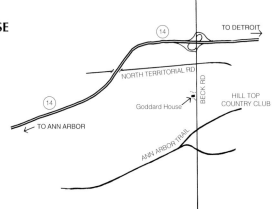

Directions: Plymouth is west of Detroit and 1.5 miles west of Interstate 275. Take Exit 18 off Route 14 (the highway between Ann Arbor and Detroit) at Beck Road south. Continue on Beck Road for 0.7 miles to the house, which is on the west side of the road. There are two large brick piers with iron gates at the entrance.

Accessibility: Only the carport can be seen through the gates and fences.

■ This red brick house, based on a rectangular grid, is close to the road. Mr Goddard and Mr Wall were friends. The Wall House is just behind it to the south and can be seen from the street through the carport of the Goddard House. The interior has been 'updated' by the current owners, but not in keeping with Wright's original intentions.

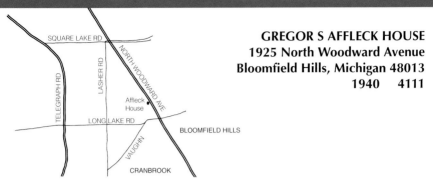

GREGOR S AFFLECK HOUSE
1925 North Woodward Avenue
Bloomfield Hills, Michigan 48013
1940   4111

Directions: The access is directly off North Woodward Avenue, one of the busy main streets heading northwest from downtown Detroit. The drive is marked with the address.

Accessibility: The house is open by appointment with limited parking in the driveway. For more information contact: The Architecture Department, Lawrence Technological Institute, 21000 West Ten Mile Road, Southfield, Michigan 48075, at least several weeks before you plan to visit .

■ The Affleck House has had a varied life having been home to several university committees. It is the interior that is renowned. Like the Pew House at Madison (p64) it is constructed on piers, although it is not often seen this way. There is a small dry pool under the living room that one might miss if it were not pointed out. The brick and horizontal board motif is similar to the Usonian Houses such as the nearby Smith House (p116) and Jacobs I House (p56), the first of this kind. The site was originally larger but parcels have been sold off. Mr Affleck was a chemical engineer who grew up in Spring Green. One of his relatives was a secretary to Wright.

MELVIN MAXWELL SMITH HOUSE
5045 Pon Valley Road
Bloomfield Hills, Michigan 48013
1949   4818

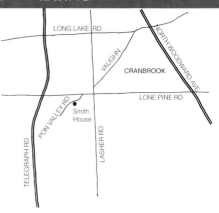

Directions: The house is just west down Lone Pine Road from Saarinen's Cranbrook, and a few blocks from the Affleck House (p115), off Lone Pine Road east of Telegraph Road. The first road going south and west of Lasher Road is Pon Valley. The house is down the hill to the south.

Accessibility: A very private site but the public facade can be seen from the road.

■ This L-shaped house is located on a fabulous site, with a lake to the south with ducks and a blue heron. Several large modern sculptures in the grounds make the house appear as a piece of sculpture itself. The clients were two school teachers who decided that, instead of spending their money on traveling the world, they would build a Wright house where the world would come to them. They were inspired to build by reading the January 1938 *Architectural Forum*, an issue devoted to Wright's work. Jack Howe later added a room at the end of the bedroom wing.

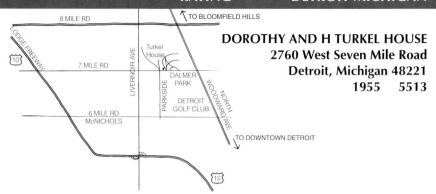

DOROTHY AND H TURKEL HOUSE
2760 West Seven Mile Road
Detroit, Michigan 48221
1955   5513

Directions: The house is on the north side of Seven Mile Road, 0.7 miles west of Woodward Avenue. Seven Mile Road is 3 miles south of 696, south on Woodward, 2.8 miles east of Lodge Freeway and 1.7 miles west of Chrysler Freeway. It is set well back on the lot and must be looked for by house number.

Accessibility: Several mature trees make a good view from the street difficult. The view up the driveway is good for understanding the unit block system.

■ The Turkel House is one of the few Usonian Automatic Houses in the Upper Great Lakes region, and was built on a common city lot. The unit block system involved economies such as clients hand manufacturing all concrete blocks to be used in construction, and acting as both general contractors and major material suppliers. Mrs Turkel read one of Wright's books, *The Natural House,* and was inspired to contact him about designing the residence. The two-story living room faces the busy street – keeping the bedrooms as far as possible from the noise. The building is 128 feet long.

WILLIAM PALMER HOUSE
227 Orchard Hills Drive
Ann Arbor, Michigan 48104
1950   5021

Directions: Very difficult to locate. Exit Route 23 at Geddes Road. Travel west 1 mile to Geddes Avenue and then proceed southwest. Geddes Avenue curves around and heads to the northwest. Orchard Hills Drive is the fifth road to the north, approximately 0.8 miles from Geddes Road. Drive north on to Orchard Hills where the house is on the east side on a corner. It is east southeast of the center of town and east of Forest Hill Cemetery on Geddes Avenue.

Accessibility: Main facade is not visible from the street.

■ As with many of the Usonian Houses, the main facade is not presented to the street. Most of the Usonian sites are landscaped in a natural way and are less formal than those of Wright's early houses. Even when these houses are in urban areas the landscaping is almost wild. Mr Palmer was a Professor of Mathematics at the University of Michigan.

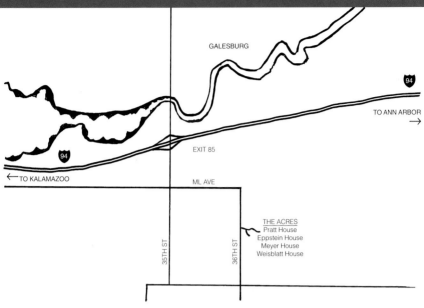

GALESBURG

94

TO ANN ARBOR
→

TO KALAMAZOO

EXIT 85

ML AVE

35TH ST

36TH ST

THE ACRES
Pratt House
Eppstein House
Meyer House
Weisblatt House

■ In 1947, a group of chemists from the Upjohn Institute commissioned Wright to design another cooperative project for a 70-acre site. The scheme involved over forty residences, each of which was allocated a circular 1-acre plot (Opus# 4828). A garden and orchard were planned for the communal areas. The clients estimated that they could afford $12,000 for each house, while Wright said that what they wanted would cost $20,000. They settled on a budget of $15,000. The initial funds came from pooling gas coupons during the war.

Circle Pines Camp (Opus# 4205), which was intended for Cloverdale (slightly north of Galesburg), was never realized, except for a single unrecognizable building at Stewart Lake. A number of the participants in this project were also involved in the Cooperative Housing for Detroit (p112). (Circle Pines Center is noted on the USGS topographic maps.)

ERIC PRATT HOUSE
11036 Hawthorne Drive
Galesburg, Michigan 49053
1948   4827

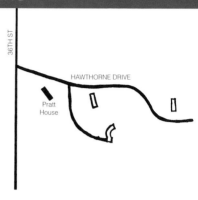

Directions: Exit Interstate 94 at mile 85. Turn south on to 35th Street and travel 0.4 miles to ML Avenue E. Turn east and travel 0.8 miles until the road ends at 36th Street. At the sign marked 'The Acres' turn south and travel 0.4 miles to Hawthorne Drive. The Pratt House is the first house on the south side of the road.

Accessibility: The house can easily be seen from street.

■ Concrete blocks were used in many of what are called the Usonian Automatic Houses. Wright's idea was that the clients would manufacture the blocks themselves in order to save money. The cavity walls were set on concrete slabs scored with the grid upon which the house was based. The grids were usually a common dimension such as 2 x 2, 2 x 4, or 4 x 4 feet. Below the concrete floor slab, set into the gravel, are heating pipes which warm the interior by radiation. The Pratts acted as the general contractor for their own house and as the general purchasing agents for the other three owners. The 2,000-square-foot house was built between 1950 and 1951.

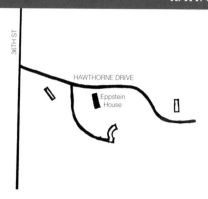

36TH ST

HAWTHORNE DRIVE

Eppstein
House

SAMUEL EPPSTEIN HOUSE
11098 Hawthorne Drive
Galesburg, Michigan 49053
1949   4905

Directions: Exit Interstate 94 at mile 85. Turn south on 35th Street and travel 0.4 miles to ML Avenue E. Turn east and travel 0.8 miles until the road ends at 36th Street. Turn south and travel 0.4 miles to Hawthorne Drive, at the sign marked 'The Acres' turn east. The Eppstein House is the second house on the south side of the road.

Accessibility: Most of the house can be seen from the road though parts are obscured by earth berms and plantings.

■ A group of chemists from the Upjohn Institute planned this development. The owners were to manufacture the blocks themselves and build their own houses. This house is dug so deeply into the hill that it almost looks as if it has sunk into it, leaving the minimum of exposed wall surface.

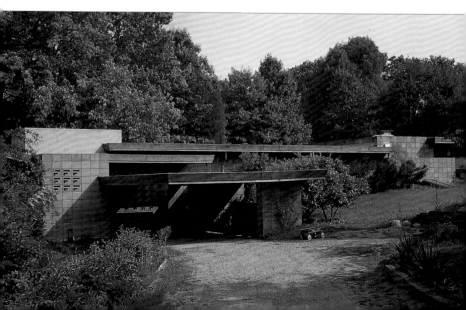

CURTIS MEYER HOUSE
11108 Hawthorne Drive
Galesburg, Michigan 49053
1950　5015

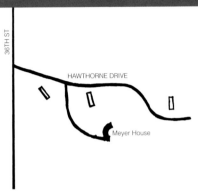

Directions: Exit Interstate 94 at mile 85. Turn south on to 35th Street and travel 0.4 miles to ML Avenue E. Turn east and travel 0.8 miles until the road ends at 36th Street. Turn south and travel 0.4 miles to Hawthorne Drive, at the sign marked 'The Acres' turn east. The Meyer House is the last house on the drive that runs south between the Pratt and Eppstein houses (pp120-121).

Accessibility: This house is at the end of a private drive. It would be disturbing to the residents to proceed down the drive.

■ This unusual house of concrete block is painted white. The wood is mahogany which is a rare choice for exterior use. The client initially used a preservative that made the wood apppear new if applied regularly. This product has now been outlawed for environmental reasons. The Meyer House is similar in many ways to the Jacobs II House (p54). The quarter circle design of the main section is set up as an arc with fifteen segments.

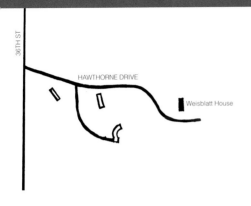

DAVID I WEISBLATT HOUSE
11185 Hawthorne Drive
Galesburg, Michigan 49053
1948   4918

36TH ST

HAWTHORNE DRIVE

Weisblatt House

Directions: Exit Interstate 94 at mile 85. Turn south on to 35th Street and travel 0.4 miles to ML Avenue E. Turn east and travel for 0.8 miles until the road ends at 36th Street. At the sign marked 'The Acres' turn south and travel 0.4 miles to Hawthorne Drive. The Weisblatt House is the last house on the north side of the road.

Accessibility: The living room can be seen from the road.

■ This house was the first of the Galesburg group to be constructed and is the last on the road. It is similar to many of the others in that the bedrooms are aligned in a straight line and entry occurs between the living room and the bedroom wing.

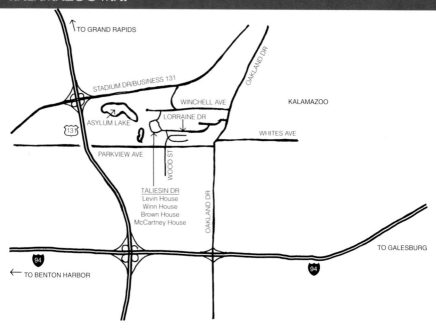

■ Many members of the Parkwyn Village Cooperative dropped out while others did not build Wright designs. The layout has been largely maintained except for the proposed community buildings at the center of the property. There are several interesting non-Wright buildings and a few that could be mistaken for designs by Wright since they are constructed from the same type of concrete block. The scheme began with circular 1-acre lots, but was redivided into irregular polygons to enable better civic management.

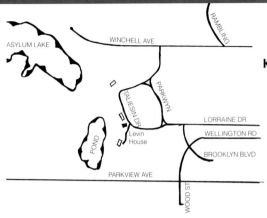

ROBERT LEVIN HOUSE
2816 Taliesin Drive
Kalamazoo, Michigan 49008
1949   4911

GPS: N 42 15.797
W 85 37.971

Directions: Exit Interstate 94 at mile 75, Oakland Drive. Go north 1.5 miles to Parkview Avenue, then west about 0.75 miles to Wood Street, then north to Lorraine Drive. Lorraine Drive west becomes Taliesin Drive. The house is on the circle drive at the corner of Taliesin Drive and a private road that leads southwest to the Winn House.

Accessibility: Overgrown plants and bushes obscure views of the house from the street. The house looks west over the lake and does not present itself to the street

■ This house is similar to the Ina Morris Harper House of St Joseph (p129) which was designed a year later. Jack Howe supervised the initial construction of all the Kalamazoo buildings and planned an addition to the house in the 1960s.

ROBERT D WINN HOUSE
2822 Taliesin Drive
Kalamazoo, Michigan 49008
1948   4815

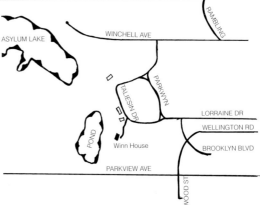

Directions: Exit Interstate 94 at mile 75, Oakland Drive. Go north 1.5 miles to Parkview Avenue and then west 0.7 miles to Wellington Road. Turn north and, keeping to the west, travel one block on to Brooklyn Boulevard, then north half a block to Lorraine Drive. Lorraine Drive west becomes Taliesin Drive. The house is at the end of the circle drive, to the west of a private drive that begins east of the Levin House.

Accessibility: Visible from the street.

■ Mr Winn was an insurance agent. The house is one in a line of similar designs for sites across the country including the Laurent House of Rockford, Illinois (p135), Pearce House of Bradbury, California, and the famous Marden House of Virginia (see East volume). In these other houses the screened porch on the west side is a terrace or patio, and is not enclosed. As with many houses for steeply sloping sites, Winn House has a second level below grade at the south end.

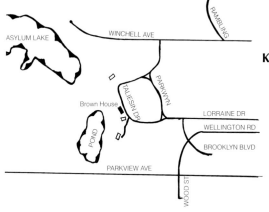

ERIC V BROWN HOUSE
2806 Taliesin Drive
Kalamazoo, Michigan 49008
1959   5003

Directions: Exit Interstate 94 at 75 Oakland Drive. Go north 1.5 miles to Parkview Avenue, then west about 0.75 miles to Wood Street, and north to Lorraine Drive. Lorraine Drive west becomes Taliesin Drive. Locate 2806 on the circle drive.

Accessibility: This and the other Kalamazoo houses are well worth the trip. A visit will show what Wright's Broadacre City proposal might have been like.

■ This large house with an elaborate plan sits on a steeply sloping site overlooking Asylum Lake to the west. Because of the slope of the site, the street elevation is minimized and the house opens up to the lake and not to the street. For this reason, little of interest can be seen from the street.

WARD McCARTNEY HOUSE
2662 Taliesin Drive
Kalamazoo, Michigan 49008
1949   4912

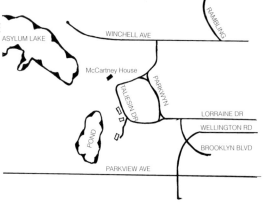

Directions: Exit Interstate 94 at 75 Oakland Drive. Go north to Parkview Avenue, then west 0.75 miles to Wood Street and north to Lorraine Drive. Lorraine Drive west becomes Taliesin Drive. The house is at the northwest corner of the circle drive, down a drive that proceeds north from the street.

Accessibility: The house is far back on the site and can only be seen by walking down the driveway. This would be disturbing to the residents.

■ Dr McCartney was a dentist. He and his new neighbor, Mr Brown, manufactured the first concrete blocks for their houses themselves. However, they found this process tedious, and later had them manufactured under contract. The house has grown since its initial construction: it began as a one-bedroomed house and now has three bedrooms and a study. Ceilings are a hardwood plywood.

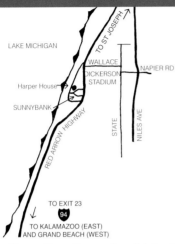

INA MORRIS HARPER HOUSE
207 Sunnybank
St Joseph, Michigan 49085
1959   5010

GPS: N 42 05.419
W 86 29.735

Directions: From the south exit Interstate 94 at mile 23 and proceed north on Red Arrow Highway for 4.5 miles to Sunnybank (across from Dickerson Stadium). Turn west toward the lake. The house is on the north side of the street at the corner.

Accessibility: The house is sited on a city lot from which one can easily see three sides of the house.

■ Overlooking the lake, the steep pitch of the living room roof reflects the light into the room when the sun is low on the water. The brick is often called 'Chicago Common' and is an inexpensive, soft brick used in many buildings throughout the Midwest. Mrs Harper had read an article by an earlier Wright client, Loren Pope, in *House Beautiful* magazine and contacted Wright for a design of her own.

CARL SCHULTZ HOUSE
2704 Highland Court
St Joseph, Michigan 49085
1957   5745

GPS: N 42 05.185
        W 86 28.716

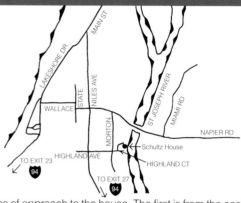

Directions: There are two directions of approach to the house. The first is from the east, passing close to Anthony House (p131). Exit Interstate 94 at mile 30 (Napier Road). Go west 3.3 miles to Miami Road and continue west on Napier, crossing the bridge and passing the hospital on the south side of the street. Travel three blocks south on either Morton Road or Niles Avenue to Highland Avenue, then east and slightly north on to Highland Court. The Schultz House is straight ahead at the end of the street. See Harper House (p129) for the west route.

Accessibility: The house can easily be seen from the driveway. There is not much more than a roof and a brick wall to see from this position.

■ This is a very large house that looks eastwards from the top of a bluff on to a city park and the St Joe River. Mr Schultz owned Benton Harbor Malleable Industries and other industrial property in the area. He was able to salvage over 50,000 bricks from these buildings and used them to limit the cost of the house to $75,000 in total.

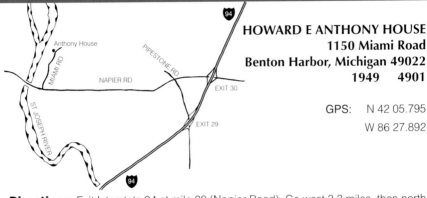

HOWARD E ANTHONY HOUSE
1150 Miami Road
Benton Harbor, Michigan 49022
1949   4901

GPS: N 42 05.795
W 86 27.892

Directions: Exit Interstate 94 at mile 30 (Napier Road). Go west 3.3 miles, then north on Miami Road for 0.7 miles. The house is on the west side of the street just before May Street.

Accessibility: The car plaza is at the entrance to the house so that any intrusion on to the terrace would be an intrusion on the occupants. The house can be seen from the trails on the flood bank below to the west though not much can be seen beyond the stone walls.

■ This a very good house that can be seen from the street. The stonework here is not as good as at Taliesin. It is one of the few house designs by Wright which includes a courtyard for cars. The house, which is based on a hexagon, has excellent views over the St Joe River and the park to the west. Howard Anthony, an electronics inventor for Heathkit, wrote to Wright to instigate the commission in 1949. The house was built soon afterwards.

ERNEST VOSBURGH HOUSE
46208 Crescent Road
Grand Beach, Michigan 49117
1916   1607

GPS: N 41 46.138
       W 86 47.960

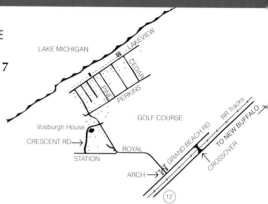

Directions: Travel 3 miles south of New Buffalo on Route 12 to the Grand Beach railroad crossover and continue south on Grand Beach Road to the arch, then west on Royal 0.2 miles to Crescent Road.

Accessibility: The house can be seen from the street. Evergreens have been planted as a privacy screen and are becoming mature, blocking most of the view.

■ This very small house is similar in many ways to the Isabel Roberts and Frank Baker (see MetroChicago volume) houses of nearly ten years earlier. The two-story living room is the main feature of the house. New window film has been added to the living room windows, obscuring the detailing of the wooden muntin patterns. Some of the new fencing and outbuildings are in discord with the Wright aesthetic.

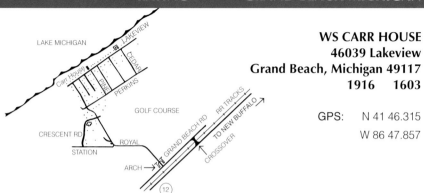

WS CARR HOUSE
46039 Lakeview
Grand Beach, Michigan 49117
1916   1603

GPS: N 41 46.315
           W 86 47.857

Directions: Exit Interstate 94 at mile 1, just north of the Michigan/Indiana State line, for Route 239 (or LaPorte Road, becoming Whittaker street in New Buffalo). Travel west for 1.5 miles to the intersection with Route 12, then turn southwest for 3 miles to the railroad crossover that connects to Grand Beach Road. Continue southwesterly to the arch for about a quarter mile from the crossover on to Royal, go all the way west to Lakeview and then northeast to 46039, which stands on the west side of the street at the corner of Pine.

Accessibility: The house is private and there is not much to see.

■ This is a four-bedroomed vacation house. The living room, at the far west end, has windows on three sides, giving the best view of Lake Michigan from the house. Nothing of substance is known about Mr Carr or his family, but most of the clients for summer houses were from the Chicago area. Other projects for Grand Beach include: a house for Miss Behn (Voight) which was planned but not built; and a house designed by Wright for Clarence Converse at Palisades Park, an unidentified location possibly near Grand Beach.

JOSEPH J BAGLEY HOUSE
47017 Lakeview
Grand Beach, Michigan 49117
1916   1601

GPS: N 41 46.401
       W 86 47.801

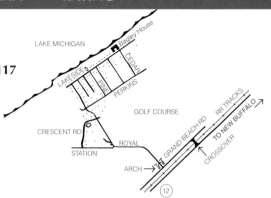

Directions: Exit Interstate 94 at mile 1, just north of the Michigan/Indiana State line, Route 239 (or LaPorte Road, becoming Whittaker Street in New Buffalo). At the intersection with Route 12, turn southwest for 3 miles to the railroad crossover that connects to Grand Beach Road. Continue southwesterly to the arch about a quarter mile from the crossover on to Royal. From here go west to Lakeview and then northeast. The house is on the west side of the street, at the corner of Cedar.

Accessibility: Street and beach viewing are possible without disturbing the occupants.

■ Having no early photos of the house, it is difficult to determine its original structure. The house has been remodeled to the point where it is almost impossible to see any of the elements usually present in a Wright building. The two-story side faces the lake to the west, with one-story wings to the east. Since the house was used only in the warm summer months, the wings were not connected by hallways but were more like pavilions linked by the roof.

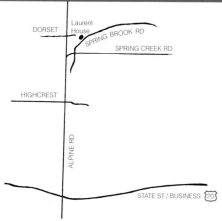

DORSET

Laurent House

SPRING BROOK RD

SPRING CREEK RD

HIGHCREST

ALPINE RD

STATE ST / BUSINESS ⟨20⟩

KENNETH LAURENT HOUSE
4646 Spring Brook Road
Rockford, Illinois 61114
1949   4814

Directions: The Laurent House is on the east side of Rockford not far from Interstate 90. Exit at mile 63 west to Alpine, then north to Spring Creek, and then travel a short distance eastwards to Spring Brook Road. The Laurent House is just after the turn from Spring Creek.

Accessibility: The house cannot be seen from road. With the window wall, any intrusion will disturb the residents.

■ Wright's designs for the Usonian Houses have many features not found in more conventional construction and design. For instance, building on a slab avoids costly deep foundations and is also at grade. This is a great advantage for the handicapped, as the original owner, Mr Laurent, could attest. He was a paraplegic in a wheelchair and needed an accessible house, which was accommodated for by Wright in his designs. The curve of the house makes it difficult to determine just how big the building is.

PETTIT MEMORIAL CHAPEL
Harrison at Webster
Belvidere, Illinois 61008
1906   0619

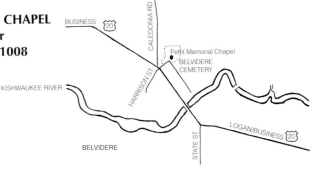

Directions: Belvidere is east of Rockford and north of Interstate 90. Exit at Genoa Road, mile 54 north to Logan, and then west into and through town. Logan takes a turn to the northwest. Cross the Kishwaukee River and after ten blocks turn northeast on to Harrison Street. At the end of the street, three blocks down, the entrance to the cemetery is on the left. The chapel is the only building inside the cemetery and is visible just past the entrance.

Accessibility: Open during daylight hours, when the cemetery is also open.

■ Emma Glassner Pettit was the sister of another Wright client, William A Glasner of Glencoe (see MetroChicago volume). The chapel was a memorial to her husband, Dr William H Pettit, a physician. After years of neglect, the chapel was restored in the 1980s. Early photos helped to identify the patterns of the art glass. The interior has a fireplace but otherwise the room is very plain. Breezes can often be felt on the porches, possibly because of the effect of the wind over and under the roof which acts like a wing.

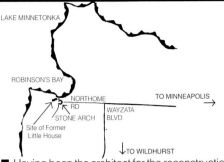

LAKE MINNETONKA

ROBINSON'S BAY

NORTHOME
RD
STONE ARCH
WAYZATA
BLVD
Site of Former
Little House

TO MINNEAPOLIS →

↓TO WILDHURST

FRANCIS W LITTLE HOUSE,
Minnetonka Boulevard,
Deephaven, Minnesota
1913   1304
Demolished 1972

■ Having been the architect for the reconstruction of the largest residential room in Wright's career, I can safely say that this is one of the saddest stories I have seen. The Little House had remained in the ownership of the same family and there seemed little reason for its demolition. When I first saw the residence, a few weeks before its scheduled relocation by the Metropolitan Museum of Art, it did not appear to be a particularly innovative structure. However, once we started to plan the reconstruction it became evident what an amazing building it actually was.

The house was designed during a difficult period in Wright's life and he seems to have been uninspired. However, when Little pointed out how dull the schemes for the art glass were, he provoked the architect into producing work of a much higher standard. A good record of these designs, and the effect of the client's input, is contained in the letters and drawings preserved at the Metropolitan.

The Little House provides one of the finest examples of Wright's understanding of landscape, and illustrates how he was able to use this knowledge to integrate his buildings with their sites. The house was perched along the ridge to the north end of the large site, and looked out north across Robinson's Bay on Lake Minnetonka. To the east of the main

house was a small summer house that Little designed and had drawn up at his utility company. This structure has also gone.

In the early 1970s, Little's daughter built a new house too close to the Wright design, and was told by the local authorities that one of the residences would have to be removed. Rather than relocating the smaller residence, or taking the new building down, she decided to demolish the older house. Luckily, after they heard the news, nearby Wright clients Don and Virginia Lovness called their friend Edgar Tafel in New York and asked for his help.

Tafel was well acquainted with many influential individuals in New York and spoke to the Director of the Metropolitan Museum of Art. As a result of this conversation, Arthur Rosenblatt, the museum's architect, decided to have the whole building dismantled and moved to New York with the exception of the library, which Tafel was able to persuade the Allentown Museum in Pennsylvania to purchase, where it is installed as a permanent exhibit.

Crates containing the building parts sat in warehouses for about ten years awaiting the completion of the Metropolitan's American Wing. Since the ceiling of this wing was nearly a foot lower than required, and the oak floor rests on bedrock, there were problems with the reconstruction. Bay windows run along the long sides of the living room. Trellises extend out from the joists of the bay's ceiling creating a cantilever that is equal in length to the bay ceiling. Both are balanced over the windows. Above this bay are clerestory windows which are held in place by steel rods that extend into what was once the attic, in the same manner as the second level of the Jacobs II House (p54).

Once the installation was complete it became one of the most popular exhibits in the entire museum. Most people's only experience of being in a Wright designed interior is visiting this room. Taking the good with the bad it would be better to have the whole building on its original site, but here at the museum a sample of Wright's work is exposed to a much larger audience.

Minnesota
- Fasbender Medical Clinic, Hastings (p26)
- Lindholm Service Station, Cloquet (p18)

Wisconsin
State sponsored tour program
- Seth Peterson Cottage, Lake Delton (p37)
- Albert D German Warehouse, Richland Center (p39)
- Taliesin, Spring Green (p42)
- Unity Chapel, Spring Green (p50)
- Monona Terrace, Madison (p58)
- Annunciation Greek Orthodox Church, Wauwatosa (p83)
- Johnson Wax Company, Racine (p91)

Michigan
- Meyer May House, Grand Rapids (p105)
- Gregor S Affleck House, Bloomfield Hills (p115)

Archives and Exhibits
- Wisconsin State Historical Society, Madison
- Milwaukee Art Museum, Milwaukee
- Northwest Architectural Archives, Minneapolis

■ Henry-Russell Hitchcock's 1942 book, *In the Nature of Materials*, was the first book I used to locate buildings. Later a college friend, Al Drap – now an architect in Fort Smith, Arkansas – gave me an updated list of Chicago addresses that started me on this twenty year trip.

John Replinger's publication, *Buildings by Frank Lloyd Wright in Six Middle Western States: Illinois, Indiana, Iowa, Michigan, Minnesota, Wisconsin*, was a source closer to home as the author was also one of my architectural instructors at the University of Illinois-Urbana, as was Walter Creese who had met and spent time with Wright. The late Bruce Goff helped me in my research by explaining what he had learned from some of Wright's contractors, thereby giving new insights into the engineering and construction of Wright's buildings.

Wilbert Hasbrouck was the publisher of the *Prairie School Review* who influenced my decision to publish the *Frank Lloyd Wright Newsletter*. I was the Director of Mr Hasbrouck's office after leaving the Illinois Central Railroad (ICG), of which Louis Sullivan's brother was Vice-President. My senior associate at ICG was Lee van Scoyoc who worked for Elmslie during the 1930s and as a result met Wright several times. He told me all he could remember about each meeting.

My interest in seeing Frank Lloyd Wright's work grew with my frequent visits to Taliesin, during which the late Olgivanna Wright, Bruce Brooks Pfeiffer, the late Wes Peters, Dick Carney and many others were gracious in their hospitality. Don and Virginia Lovness, who invited me to stay at their compound, shared many wonderful stories from the years they enjoyed as part of the 'inner circle' at Taliesin.

Olgivanna Lloyd Wright's book, *Frank Lloyd Wright: His Life, His Work, His Words*, included a more complete listing of Wright's work and has been helpful. The Opus Numbers listing included by Bruce Pfeiffer in the five-volume set edited by Anthony Alofsin is the most valuable and complete listing of Wright's work, which covers all buildings, remodelings, projects, and many individual decorative designs. This list is the first place to look for confirmation of built and unbuilt buildings, and can also be used to track not only the drawings, but also the art glass, furniture, and other moveable objects.

William Allin Storrer's work, *The Frank Lloyd Wright Companion*, was helpful in clarifying many things about Wright and publishing. Storrer put in a tremendous amount of work and travel to produce his books, and his firsthand experience will be very valuable to many. Dale Northup's book *Frank Lloyd Wright in Michigan* brought together much information not to be found elsewhere.

Mary Jane Hamilton should put her work into a major volume as it has been very helpful to many people already. Narciso Menocal of the University of Wisconsin has been generous with both hospitality and ideas since our first meeting at the University of Illinois. Brian Spencer has a gift for locating information and materials that would be informative to many if he would only publish it.

The Prairie Archives at the Milwaukee Art Museum, started by Brian Spencer in the late 1970s, is still a little-tapped source of a considerable amount of primary information centering on the Niedecken-Wallbridge firm. The Northwest Architectural Archives and Al Lathrop are other overlooked treasure-troves of original material. The Minneapolis Public Library Reference Department dug out many old files which answered numerous questions about events in the 1920s. The Northwestern University Map Library assisted with their full set of Geological Survey and Nautical maps.

Paul Sprague has been a constant inspiration since our first meeting at his office in the Glasner House. Jack Howe's patience in answering so many questions about Wright had no limits. He and his wife were so gracious with their hospitality, both in Burnsville and Taliesin, that I cannot thank them enough.

I want to thank Mike Reid of Lansing, as well as his son and daughter, for the tour of Cedarville and Marquette Island he provided. Dave from the Carolyn Beach Motel in Thessalon, near Sapper Island, provided very useful guidance. I thank my brothers Jerry, Bill and John for having the patience to stop off at Desbarats prior to our weeks of walleye fishing.

Wright clients who made my travels a pleasure include the late Melvin Maxwell Smith and his wife Sara, who on many occasions over the past twenty years gave me a much deeper understanding of life in a Wright house. Their company was always difficult to leave. Dr LaFond opened his house for a brief but thorough inspection. Barbara Elsner has been patient and generous with my frequent visits to her beautiful house. Irma Marlin and her late son, Bill, were generous with their time and with information, while the gracious Palmers hosted an impromptu visit from Sara Smith and myself. Balthazar Korab related his early experiences in investigating and photographing Wright buildings.

Jim and Kim Malnight have hosted me on many of my frequent trips to Grand Rapids and I am ever grateful for the counsel and encouragement of Bob Waters, Marie, Don Bins and Tom Rafool from Porters of Racine. Phil and Sandra Ellegard Mattison of Delavan who introduced me to their neighbors, and Bob Grotters and Ryan Kanis of Klingman's Furniture store, Grand Rapids, brought a new perspective to my work.

Scot Gilmore, Mark Mackintosh, Dave O'Connor, Faith Weimer, Mindy Baird and Nancy Forbes have contributed to the writing of this book. Tom Homer provided much for this work. Jack Boyko should also receive thanks.

Sam Johnson and his staff at Johnson Wax spent a great deal of time helping me to understand complex buildings and events. Dick Kinch and many others at Wingspread, The Johnson Foundation, have been so kind to me, for which I am grateful. Jonathan Lipman and the Frank Lloyd Wright Building Conservancy keep me informed about events and information through their quarterly newsletter.

Thanks to the late Bruce Goff, the Harders, and *Architectural Digest* for sending me to Minnesota to do the story on the Harder House, and Bill Hooper who introduced me to the GPS and lent me his unit.

If it were not for the hard work put into this project by John Stoddart, Managing Director of Academy Group Ltd, this book would not have seen the light of day. I also thank his staff, including Andrea Bettella, Maggie Toy, Rachel Bean, Stephen James Watt and Ellie Duffy, who brought the book to life. Thanks also to Marianne Bohr who helped to get the project started. I am most appreciative of the efforts of all involved and hope this team will remain together in order to produce more of these quality publications.

My family is a constant source of inspiration and my little sister Mary keeps me informed of many events in Minnesota. Ann Terando has been very helpful in many ways. Thank you.

Books

■ Mary Ellen Chase, *A Goodly Fellowship*, The Macmillan Co (New York), 1939.

A short chapter in this book is devoted to the experiences of the author when she attended Hillside Home School which was run by Wright's aunts, Nell and Jane.

■ Henry-Russell Hitchcock, *In the Nature of Materials*, Duell, Sloan and Pearce (New York), 1942.

Even with the last twenty years missing, this is still the best single volume on Wright's work. The list of buildings is consistently the most accurate and it remains a most valuable resource.

■ John Replinger and Allan Frumkin, *Buildings by Frank Lloyd Wright in Six Middle Western States: Illinois, Indiana, Iowa, Michigan, Minnesota, Wisconsin*, The Art Institute of Chicago (Chicago), 1949.

Based upon Hitchcock's 1942 list, this book contains valuable and updated information but still misses the last ten years of Wright's life. It was a small publication and is not in general circulation.

■ Edgar Kaufmann and Ben Raeburn eds, *Frank Lloyd Wright: Writings & Buildings*, Meridian Books (New York), 1960.

Besides essential material on the published writings, this book contains the first full list of buildings and projects.

■ Maginel Wright Barney, *The Valley of God-Almighty Joneses*, Appelton-Century (New York), 1965.

Frank Lloyd Wright's sister wrote this historical look at the Lloyd Jones family and its journey from Wales to Wisconsin.

■ Olgivanna Lloyd Wright, *Frank Lloyd Wright: His Life, His Work, His Words*, Horizon Press (New York), 1966.

This book contains a list of Wright's work and accomplishments in an appendix that is still useful today.

■ Leonard K Eaton, *Two Chicago Architects and Their Clients*, The MIT Press (Cambridge, Massachusetts), 1969.

Short biographies of several Wright clients are presented in this volume, including Meyer May of Grand Rapids and Eugene Gilmore of Madison.

■ Wayne Andrews, *Architecture in Chicago and Midwest*, Athenaeum (New York), 1970.
A chapter is devoted to Wright and a few others associated with the Prairie School. The descriptions are more casual than usual and provide information not included in other publications.

■ H Allen Brooks, *The Prairie School: Frank Lloyd Wright and His Midwest Contemporaries*, University of Toronto Press (Toronto), 1972.
This book presents probably the finest work on the buildings of Wright and his associates. It also provides a good account of how the new American architecture grew and died.

■ John Sergeant, *Frank Lloyd Wright's Usonian Houses*, Whitney Library of Design, Watson Guptil (New York), 1976.
Considering the quality of the descriptions included, one wishes that the book were two or three times longer and included more of Wright's buildings and projects.

■ Herbert and Katherine Jacobs, *Building with Frank Lloyd Wright: An Illustrated Memoir*, Chronicle Books (New York), 1978.
Two of the most significant buildings built during Wright's Usonian period were for the Jacobs, and this publication provides an excellent illustrated account of their design. The cover photograph is another reminder of how elementary Wright's designs are.

■ Robert L Sweeney, *Frank Lloyd Wright: An Annotated Bibliography*, Hennessey & Ingalls (Los Angeles), 1978.
Virtually every publication on Wright and his buildings are noted in this excellent work, and there is an index, by building name, provided for those interested in a more historical background. One hopes that an updated volume is planned for the future.

■ Anthony Alofsin ed, *Frank Lloyd Wright: An Index to the Taliesin Correspondence*, Garland Press (New York), 1983.
The microfilm letters to and from Frank Lloyd Wright are indexed and cross-referenced within these five volumes. The definitive list of Wright's work compiled by Bruce Brooks Pfeiffer, the Taliesin archivist, often referred to as the Opus Numbers, is also included in this work. The Opus list would be even more valuable if updated and published separately.

■ Patrick J Meehan, *Frank Lloyd Wright: A Guide to Archival Sources*, Garland (New York), 1983.
This publication not only lists the locations of the archival sources but also includes fine summaries of the contents. It is not widely known.

■ Walter L Creese, *The Crowning of the American Landscape: Eight Great Spaces and Their Buildings,* Princeton University Press (Princeton, New Jersey), 1985.

A considerable amount of new information about the history and background of Taliesin is provided within this text, however, there are still many questions that remain unanswered. The definitive work on the valley has yet to be published.

■ Shirley du Fresne McArthur, *Frank Lloyd Wright, American System Built Homes in Milwaukee,* North Point Historical Society (Milwaukee), 1985.

This book provides a full discussion of the American Systems project and the major protagonists involved.

■ Jonathan Lipman, *Frank Lloyd Wright and the Johnson Wax Buildings,* Rizzoli (New York), 1986.

A full discussion of all of the buildings designed and built for the Johnsons is covered in this publication. Construction photographs and drawings are included.

■ A Dale Northup, *Frank Lloyd Wright in Michigan,* Reference Publications Inc (Algonac, Michigan), 1991.

Most of the buildings and some of the projects for Michigan are discussed in this book. Several exceptional explanatory drawings are included.

■ Thomas A Heinz, *Frank Lloyd Wright,* Monograph 18, Academy Editions (London), 1992.

This publication provides alternative descriptions of many of Wright's buildings.

■ William Allin Storrer, *The Frank Lloyd Wright Companion,* University of Chicago Press (Chicago and London), 1993.

A considerable amount of work went into the assembly of this book, and it features plans for almost every Wright building ever built. Mr Storrer has included expansive information on many little known clients as well as providing an architectural commentary.

■ Neil Levine, *The Architecture of Frank Lloyd Wright,* Princeton University Press (Princeton, New Jersey), 1996.

A few major works are highlighted and discussed in great detail in this text; the analysis of which encompasses many lesser designs. There is a considerable amount of new information which helps to clarify some previously obscure facts.

Periodicals

■ Walter Schmidt, 'Catherine Tobin Wright's Scrapbook', *Frank Lloyd Wright Newsletter* (Evanston), vol 3; no 4, Fourth Quarter 1980, pp4-8.

Some rare views of the Taliesin and Oak Park buildings are illustrated here.

■ Patrick J Meehan, 'Frank Lloyd Wright's Lake Geneva Hotel', *Frank Lloyd Wright Newsletter* (Evanston), vol 4; no 2, Second Quarter 1981, pp6-10.

This documents the full story of the life and death of the hotel.

■ John O Holzhueter, 'Frank Lloyd Wright's Designs for Robert Lamp', *Wisconsin Magazine of History*, Wisconsin Historical Society (Madison), vol 72; no 2, Winter 1988-1989, pp82-125.

It would be beneficial to have the high level of scholarship presented in each of these three articles applied to all of the Wright buildings and projects; perhaps an endowment for Mr Holzhueter is in order to accomplish this. Mr Lamp was always a bit of a mystery, as was the unusual design for his house, and so many obstinate questions are fully answered in this complete discussion.

■ John O Holzhueter, 'Cudworth Beye, Frank Lloyd Wright, and the Yahara River Boathouse, 1905', *Wisconsin Magazine of History*, Wisconsin Historical Society (Madison), vol 72; no 3, Spring 1989, pp162-198.

The misconceptions about the origins of this significant project are corrected in this article. A short note at the end of the piece makes note of the serendipity that enters into the hard work of the scholar.

■ John O Holzhueter, 'Frank Lloyd Wright's 1893 Boathouse Designs for Madison's Lakes', *Wisconsin Magazine of History*, Wisconsin Historical Society (Madison), vol 72; no 4, Summer 1989, pp273-291.

Many people were unsure of the location of the Mendota Boathouse and the story behind the first design for Lake Monona. This article closes those gaps.

Key

UGL	Upper Great Lakes
W	West
E	East
MC	MetroChicago

	Vol	Date	Opus	Page
Ablin, George, Bakersfield, Calif.	W	1958	5812	
Adams, Harry S, Oak Park, Ill.	MC	1913	1301	
Adams, Mary MW, Highland Park, Ill.	MC	1905	0501	
Adams, William, Chicago, Ill.	MC	1900	0001	
Adelman, Albert, Fox Point, Wisc.	UGL	1948	4801	78
Adelman, Benjamin, Phoenix, Ariz.	W	1951	5101	
Affleck, Gregor S, Bloomfield Hills, Mich.	UGL	1940	4111	115
Airplane House – see Gilmore.	UGL	1908	0806	57
Allen, Henry J, Wichita, Kansas.	W	1917	1701	
Allentown Art Museum, Little House Library.	E/UGL	1978	1304	137
Alpaugh, Amy, Northport, Mich.	UGL	1947	4703	99
Alsop, Caroll, Oskaloosa, Iowa.	W	1948	4804	
Amberg, JH, Grand Rapids, Mich.	UGL	1910	1001	106
American Systems Buildings – see Richards.	UGL	1916	1606	79
Anderton Court, Los Angeles, Beverly Hills, Calif.	W	1952	5032	
Angster, Herbert, Lake Bluff, Ill.	MC	1911	1101	
Annunciation Greek Orthodox Church, Wauwatosa, Wisc.	UGL	1956	5611	83
Anthony, Howard E, Benton Harbor, Mich.	UGL	1949	4901	131
Arizona Biltmore Hotel, Phoenix, Ariz.	W	1927	2710	
Armstrong, Andrew F, Ogden Dunes, Ind.	E	1939	3901	
Arnold, E Clarke, Columbus, Wisc.	UGL	1954	5401	66
Auldbrass, Stevens Plantation, Yemassee, SC.	E	1940	4015	
Austin, Charlcey, Greenville, SC.	E	1951	5102	
Bach, Emil, Chicago, Ill.	MC	1915	1501	
Baghdad Projects, Iraq.	W	1957	5748	
Bagley, Frederick, Hinsdale, Ill.	MC	1894	9401	
Bagley, Joseph J, Grand Beach, Mich.	UGL	1916	1601	134

Baird, Theodore, Amherst, Mass.	E	1940	4001	
Baker, Frank J, Wilmette, Ill.	MC	1909	0901	
Balch, Oscar B, Oak Park, Ill.	MC	1911	1102	
Baldwin, Hiram, Kenilworth, Ill.	MC	1905	0502	
Banff National Park Pavilion, Canada.	W	1911	1302	
Bannerstone House – see Dana, Susan Lawrence.	E	1904	9905	
Barnsdall, Aline, Hollyhock House,				
Los Angeles, Calif.	W	1920	1705	
Studio Residence A.	W	1920	2002	
Studio Residence B.	W	1920	2003	
Kindergarten, Little Dipper.	W	1921	2301	
Barton, George, Buffalo, NY.	E	1903	0301	
Bassett, Dr HW, Oak Park, Ill, site.	MC	1894	9402	
Bazett, Sidney, Hillsborough, Calif.	W	1940	4002	
Beach Cottages, Egypt, site.	E	1927	2711	
Beachy, Peter, Oak Park, Ill.	MC	1906	0601	
Berger, Robert, San Anselmo, Calif.	W	1950	5039	
Beth Sholom Synagogue, Elkins Park, Penn.	E	1954	5313	
Bitter Root Inn, Darby, Montana, site.	W	1909	0918	
Blair, Quinton, Cody, Wyoming.	W	1952	5203	
Blossom, George, Chicago, Ill.	MC	1892	9201	
Bogk, Frederick C, Milwaukee, Wisc.	UGL	1916	1602	85
Boomer, Jorgine, Phoenix, Ariz.	W	1953	5302	
Booth, Sherman, House, Glencoe, Ill.	MC	1915	1502	
Cottage.	MC	1911	1119	
Development.	MC	1915	1505	
Kier, William F.	MC	1915	1516	
Kissam, Lute F.	MC	1915	1516	
Perry, Charles R.	MC	1915	1516	
Root, Hollis R.	MC	1915	1516	
Ross, William F.	MC	1915	1516	
Boswell, William P, Indian Hill, Ohio.	E	1957	5704	
Bott, Frank, Kansas City, Mo.	W	1956	5627	
Boulter, Cedric G, Cincinnati, Ohio.	E	1954	5403	
Boynton, Edward E, Rochester, NY.	E	1908	0801	
Bradley, R Harley, Kankakee, Ill.	E	1900	0002	

Bramson Dress Shop, Oak Park, Ill, site.	MC	1937	3706	
Brandes, Ray, Issaquah, Washington.	W	1952	5204	
Brauner, Erling, Okemos, Mich.	UGL	1948	4601	109
Brigham, Edmund F, Glencoe, Ill.	MC	1915	1503	
Brown, Charles A, Evanston, Ill.	MC	1905	0503	
Brown, Eric V, Kalamazoo, Mich.	UGL	1959	5003	127
Brownes Bookstore, Chicago.	MC	1907	0802	
Bubilian, AH, Rochester, Minn.	UGL	1947	4709	29
Buehler, Maynard P, Orinda, Calif.	W	1948	4805	
Burleigh, Lewis, Wilmette, Ill.	MC	1917	1506	
Carlson, Raymond, Phoenix, Ariz.	W	1950	5004	
Carr, John O, Glenview, Ill.	MC	1950	5014	
Carr, WS, Grand Beach, Mich.	UGL	1916	1603	133
Cass, William, New York City, Staten Island, NY.	E	1959	5518	
Chahroudi, AK, Lake Mahopac, New York, NY.	E	1951	5104	
Charnley, James, Chicago, Ill.	MC	1891	9001	
Ocean Springs, Miss.	E	1890	9101	
Cheney, Edwin H, Oak Park, Ill.	MC	1904	0401	
Christian, John E, West Lafayette, Ind.	E	1954	5405	
Christie, James B, Bernardsville, NJ.	E	1940	4003	
Circle Pines Resort, Cloverdale, Mich, site.	UGL	1942	4205	119
City National Bank & Hotel,				
Mason City, Iowa.	W	1909	0902	
Clark, W Irving, LaGrange, Ill.	MC	1893	9209	
Community Church, Kansas City, Mo.	W	1940	4004	
Como Orchard, Darby, Mont, site.	W	1910	1002	
Cooke, Andrew, Virginia Beach, Virginia.	E	1953	5219	
Coonley, Avery, Riverside, Ill.	MC	1908	0803	
Coonley Playhouse, Riverside, Ill.	MC	1912	1201	
Copeland, William H, Oak Park, Ill.	MC	1909	0904	
Crystal Heights, Washington DC, site.	E	1939	4016	
Cummings Real Estate, River Forest, Ill, site.	MC	1907	0702	
Currier Gallery of Art, Zimmerman House,				
Manchester, NH.	E	1950	5214	
Dallas, Theater Center.	W	1955	5514	
Dana, Susan Lawrence, Springfield, Ill.	E	1904	9905	

Davenport, E Arthur, River Forest, Ill.	MC	1901	0101
Davidson, Walter V, Buffalo, NY.	E	1908	0804
Davis, Richard, Marion, Indiana.	E	1950	5037
Death Valley, Calif, Johnson & Wright, sites.	W	1921	2306
Deephaven – see Little, Francis W.	UGL	1913	1304	137
Library, Allentown, Penn.	E/UGL	1978	1304	137
Metropolitan Museum, New York, NY.	E/UGL	1982	1304	137
Deertrack – see Roberts, Abby.	UGL	1936	3603	97
DeRhodes, KC, South Bend, Ind.	E	1906	0602
Dobkins, John J, Canton, Ohio	E	1954	5407
Duncan, Don, Lisle, Ill.	MC	1957	5518
Edwards, James, Okemos, Mich.	UGL	1949	4904	110
Elam, SP, Austin, Minn.	UGL	1951	5105	30
Emmond, Robert G, LaGrange, Ill.	MC	1892	9202
Ennis, Charles, Los Angeles, Calif.	W	1924	2401
Erdman Prefab houses.			
Iber, Frank, Plover, Wisc.	UGL	1957	5518	34
Jackson, Arnold, Beaver Dam, Wisc.	UGL	1957	5518	67
LaFond, Dr Edward, St Joseph, Minn.	UGL	1960	5518	20
McBean, James, Rochester, Minn.	UGL	1957	5706	27
Mollica, Joseph, Bayside, Wisc.	UGL	1958	5518	77
Rudin, Walter, Madison.	UGL	1957	5706	61
Van Tamlen, Eugene, Madison.	UGL	1956	5518	60
Erdman Prefab houses.			
Duncan, Lisle, Ill.	MC	1957	5518
Post, Barrington, Ill.	MC	1957	5518
Erdman Prefab houses.			
Cass, New York City, NY.	E	1959	5518
Zaferiou, Blauvelt, NY.	E	1961	5518
Eppstein, Samuel, Galesburg, Mich.	UGL	1949	4905	121
Euchtman, Joseph, Baltimore, Maryland.	E	1940	4005
Evans, Raymond W, Chicago, Ill.	MC	1908	0805
Exhibition House, New York City, NY, site.	E	1953	5314
E-Z Polish Factory, Chicago, Ill.	MC	1905	0504
Fabyan, George, Geneva, Ill.	MC	1907	0703
Fallingwater – see Kaufmann, Edgar.	E	1936	3602

Fasbender Medical Clinic, Hastings, Minn.	UGL	1957	5730	26
Fawcett, Randall, Los Banos, Calif.	W	1955	5418	
Feiman, Ellis A, Canton, Ohio.	E	1954	5408	
Fir Tree, Friedman, Pecos, NM.	W	1952	4512	
Florida Southern College, Lakeland, Fla.	E	1938	3805	
Pfeiffer Chapel.	E	1938	3805	
Roux Library.	E	1941	3805	
Seminar Buildings.	E	1940	3805	
Industrial Arts Building.	E	1942	3805	
Administration Building.	E	1945	3805	
Science Building.	E	1953	3805	
Danforth Chapel.	E	1954	3805	
Fountainhead, Hughes, Jackson, Miss.	E	1949	4908	
Foster, Stephen A, Chicago, Ill.	MC	1900	0003	
Fox River Country Club, Geneva, Ill.	MC	1907	0704	
Francis Apartments, Chicago, Ill, site.	MC	1895	9501	
Francisco Terrace (formerly Chicago now parts moved to Oak Park).	MC	1895	9502	
Frederick, Louis B, Barrington Hills, Ill.	MC	1954	5426	
Freeman, Samuel, Los Angeles, Calif.	W	1923	2402	
Freeman, WH, Hinsdale, Ill.	MC	1903	0312	
Fricke, William G, Oak Park, Ill.	MC	1901	0201	
Friedman, Allen, Bannockburn, Ill.	MC	1956	5624	
Friedman, Arnold, Pecos, NM.	W	1945	4512	
Friedman, Sol, Pleasantville, New York, NY.	E	1949	4906	
Fuller, Grace, Glencoe, Ill, site.	MC	1906	0603	
Fuller, Welbie, Pass Christian, Miss, site.	E	1951	5106	
Fukuhara, Arinobu, Hakone, Japan.	W	1918	1801	
Furbeck, George, Oak Park, Ill.	MC	1897	9701	
Furbeck, Rollin, Oak Park, Ill.	MC	1897	9801	
Gakuen School, Tokyo, Japan.	W	1921	2101	
Gale, Thomas H, Oak Park, Ill.	MC	1892	9203	
Gale, Summer House, Whitehall, Mich.	UGL	1897	0522	101
Gale, Mrs Thomas H, Oak Park, Ill.	MC	1909	0905	
Gale, Cottages, Whitehall, Mich.	UGL	1905	0502	102
Gale, Walter M, Oak Park, Ill.	MC	1893	9302	

Galesburg Country Home Acres, Mich.	UGL	1948	4828	119
Gammage Memorial Auditorium, Tempe, Ariz.	W	1959	5904	
German Warehouse, Richland Center, Wisc.	UGL	1915	1504	39
Gerts, George, Duplex, Whitehall, Mich.	UGL	1902	0202	104
Gerts, Walter, Cottage, Whitehall, Mich.	UGL	1902	0203	103
Gerts, Walter, River Forest, Ill, site.	MC	1911	1114	
Gillin, John A, Dallas, Texas.	W	1950	5034	
Gilmore, Eugene A, Madison, Wisc.	UGL	1908	0806	57
Glasner, William A, Glencoe, Ill.	MC	1905	0505	
Glenlloyd – see Bradley, R Harley.	E	1900	0002	
Glore, Lake Forest, Ill.	MC	1951	5107	
Goan, Peter, LaGrange, Ill.	MC	1893	9403	
Goddard, Lewis H, Plymouth, Mich.	UGL	1953	5317	114
Goetsch-Winkler, Okemos, Mich.	UGL	1939	3907	108
Goodrich, Harry C, Oak Park, Ill.	MC	1896	9601	
Gordon, Conrad E, Wilsonville, Oregon.	W	1957	5710	
Grady Gammage Auditorium, Tempe, Ariz.	W	1959	5904	
Grant, Douglas, Cedar Rapids, Iowa.	W	1946	4503	
Graycliff, Martin D, Derby, NY.	E	1927	2701	
Greek Orthodox Church, Wauwatosa, Wisc.	UGL	1956	5611	83
Greenberg, Maurice, Dousman, Wisc.	UGL	1954	5409	75
Greene, William B, Aurora, Ill.	MC	1912	1203	
Gridley, AW, Batavia, Ill.	MC	1906	0604	
Griggs, Chauncey L, Tacoma, Wash.	W	1946	4604	
Guggenheim Museum, New York, NY.	E	1956	4305	
Hagan, Isaac Newton, Ohiopyle, Penn.	E	1954	4510	
Hanna, Paul, Palo Alto, Calif.	W	1937	3701	
Hardy, Thomas P, Racine, Wisc.	UGL	1905	0506	94
Harlan, Dr Allison, Chicago, Ill, site.	MC	1892	9204	
Harper, Ina Morris, St Joseph, Mich.	UGL	1959	5010	129
Hayashi, Aisaku, Tokyo, Japan.	W	1917	1702	
Haynes, John, Fort Wayne, Ind.	E	1951	5110	
Heath, William R, Buffalo, NY.	E	1905	0507	
Hebert, AW, Evanston, Ill.	MC	1902	0112	
Davis Street.	MC	1902		
Ashland Avenue.	MC	1902		

Heller, Isadore, Chicago, Ill.	MC	1896	9606	
Henderson, FB, Elmhurst, Ill.	MC	1901	0104	
Heurtley, Arthur, Oak Park, Ill.	MC	1902	0204	
Summer Cottage, Marquette Island, Mich.	UGL	1902	0214	98
Hickox, Warren, Kankakee, Ill.	E	1900	0004	
Hills, Edward R, Oak Park, Ill.	MC	1906	0102	
Hillside Home School, Taliesin,				
Spring Green, Wisc.	UGL	1902	0216	46
Hoffman, Max, Rye, New York, NY.	E	1955	5535	
Hoffman Showroom, New York, NY.	E	1956	5622	
Hollyhock House – see Barnsdall, Aline.	W	1920	1705	
Home and Studio, Oak Park, Ill – see				
Wright, Frank Lloyd.	MC	1889	8901	
Honeycomb House – see Hanna, Paul.	W	1937	3701	
Horner, LK, Chicago, Ill, site.	MC	1908	0807	
Horshoe Inn, Estes Park, Colo, site.	W	1908	0814	
Hoyt, PD, Geneva, Ill.	MC	1906	0605	
Hughes, J Willis, Jackson, Miss.	E	1949	4908	

Hillside Home School, Taliesin, Spring Green, Wisc, c1930

Humphries Theater, Dallas, Texas.	W	1955	5514	
Hunt, Stephen MB, LaGrange, Ill.	MC	1907	0705	
Hunt, Stephen MB, Oshkosh, Wisc.	UGL	1917	1703	35
Husser, Joseph, Chicago, site.	MC	1899	9901	
Iber, Frank, Plover, Wisc.	UGL	1957	5518	34
Imperial Hotel, Tokyo, Japan, original site.	W	1915	1509	
Imperial Hotel Reconstruction, Nagoya, Japan.	W	1976	1509	
Ingalls, J Kibben, River Forest, Ill.	MC	1909	0906	
Irving, Edward P, Decatur, Ill.	E	1910	1003	
Jackson, Arnold, Beaver Dam, formerly Madison, Wisc.	UGL	1957	5518	67
Jacobs, Herbert, I, Madison, Wisc.	UGL	1936	3702	56
Jacobs, Herbert, II, Middleton, Wisc.	UGL	1948	4812	54
Jiyu Gakuen School, Japan.	W	1921	2101	
Johnson, AP, Delavan, Wisc.	UGL	1905	0508	74
Johnson, Herbert F, Wingspread, Wind Point, Wisc.	UGL	1937	3703	88
Johnson, Oscar C, Evanston, Ill.	MC	1917	1506	

Herbert Jacobs I House, Madison, Wisc, c1938

Johnson Wax Company, Racine, Wisc.	UGL	1936	3601	91
Jones, Fred B, Delavan, Wisc.	UGL	1900	0103	72
Gatehouse	UGL	1900	0103	71
Jones, Richard Lloyd, Tulsa, Okla.	W	1929	2902	
Juvenile Cultural Center, Wichita, Kansas.	W	1957	5743	
Kalil, Toufik, Manchester, NH.	E	1955	5506	
Kansas City Community Christian Church.	W	1040	4004	
Kaufmann, Edgar, Fallingwater, Mill Run, Penn.	E	1936	3602	
Kaufmann Office, now London, England.	E	1937	3704	
Keland, Willard H, Racine, Wisc.	UGL	1954	5417	90
Keys, Thomas E, Rochester, Minn.	UGL	1950	5012	28
Kier, William F, Glencoe, Ill.	MC	1915	1516	
Kinney, Patrick, Lancaster, Wisc.	UGL	1951	5038	38
Kinney, Sterling, Amarillo, Texas.	W	1957	5717	
Kissam, Daniel, Glencoe, Ill.	MC	1915	1516	
Kraus, Russell, Kirkwood, Mo.	W	1951	5123	
Kundert Medical Clinic, San Luis Obispo, Calif.	W	1956	5614	
LaFond, Dr Edward, St Joseph, Minn.	UGL	1960	5518	20
Lake Delavan Yacht Club, Delavan, Wisc, site.	UGL	1904	0217	68
Lake Geneva Hotel, Lake Geneva, Wisc, site.	UGL	1912	1202	68
Lake Tahoe Summer Colony, site.	W	1922	2205	
Lamberson, Jack, Oskaloosa, Iowa.	W	1947	4712	
La Miniatura, Millard, Alice, Pasadena, Calif.	W	1923	2302	
Lamp, Robert M, Madison, Wisc.	UGL	1903	0402	59
Lamp, Robert M, Rockyroost, Madison, Wisc, site.	UGL	1893	9301	58
Larkin Building, Buffalo, NY, site.	E	1903	0403	
Laurent, Kenneth, Rockford, Ill.	UGL	1949	4814	135
Laurent, Kenneth, Rockford, Ill.	MC	1949	4814	
Lawrence Memorial Library, Springfield, Ill.	E	1905	0509	
Levin, Robert, Kalamazoo, Mich.	UGL	1949	4911	125
Lewis, George, Talahassee, Fla.	E	1952	5207	
Lewis, Lloyd, Libertyville, Ill.	MC	1940	4008	
Lincoln Center, Abraham, Chicago, Ill.	MC	1903	0010	
Lindholm, RW, Cloquet, Minn.	UGL	1952	5208	19
Lindholm Service Station, Cloquet, Minn.	UGL	1957	5739	18
Little, Francis W, Peoria, Ill.	E	1902	0009	

Original site, Deephaven, Minn.	UGL	1913	1304	137
Living Room, Metropolitan Museum of Art, New York City, NY.	E/UGL	1982	1304	137
Library, Allentown Museum of Art, Penn.	E/UGL	1978	1304	137
Little Dipper, Barnsdall, Los Angeles, Calif.	W	1921	2301	
Lockridge Medical Clinic, Whitefish, Montana.	W	1958	5813	
Lovness, Donald, House, Stillwater, Minn.	UGL	1955	5507	24
Lovness, Donald, Cottage, Stillwater, Minn.	UGL	1974	5824	25
Lykes, Norman, Phoenix, Arizona.	W	1966	5908	
MacHarg, William, Chicago, Ill, site.	MC	1891	9002	
Manson, Charles L, Wausau, Wisc.	UGL	1940	4009	32
Marcus, Stanley, Dallas, Texas, site.	W	1935	3501	
Marden, Louis, McLean, Va.	E	1952	5220	
Marin County Civic Center, San Rafel, Calif.	W	1957	5746	
Martin, Darwin D, Buffalo, NY.	E	1904	0405	
Martin, DD, Gardeners Cottage, Buffalo, NY.	E	1905	0530	
Martin Graycliffe, Derby, New York, NY.	E	1927	2701	
Martin, William E, Oak Park, Ill.	MC	1902	0304	

Lake Geneva Hotel, Lake Geneva, Wisc, c1970

Mathews, Arthur C, Atherton, Calif.	W	1950	5013	
May, Meyer, Grand Rapids, Mich.	UGL	1908	0817	105
McArthur, Warren, Chicago, Ill.	MC	1892	9205	
McBean, James B, Rochester, Minn.	UGL	1957	5706	27
McCartney, Ward, Kalamazoo, Mich.	UGL	1949	4912	128
McCormick, Harold, Lake Forest, Ill, site.	MC	1907	0713	
Meier, Delbert W, Monona, Iowa.	W	1917	1506	
Meiji Mura Museum, Imperial Hotel, Japan.	W	1915	1509	
Mendota Boathouse, Madison, Wisc, site.	UGL	1893	9304	58
Metropolitan Museum of Art, Little House, Living Room, New York City, NY.	E/UGL	1982	1304	137
Meyer, Curtis, Galesburg, Mich.	UGL	1950	5015	122
Meyers Medical Clinic, Dayton, Ohio.	E	1956	5613	
Midway Gardens, Chicago, Ill, site.	MC	1914	1401	
Millard, George M, Highland Park, Ill.	MC	1906	0606	
Millard, Alice, Pasadena, Calif.	W	1923	2302	
Miller, Alvin, Charles City, Iowa.	W	1946	5016	
Miller, Arthur and Marilyn Monroe, site.	E	1957	5719	
Moe, Ingwald, Gary, Ind.	MC	1908	0539	
Mollica, Joseph, Bayside, Wisc.	UGL	1958	5518	77
Moore, Nathan G, Oak Park, Ill.	MC	1895	9503	
Monona Terrace, Madison, site.	UGL	1938	3909	58
Monroe, Marilyn and Arthur Miller, site	E	1957	5719	
Mori Art Shop, Chicago, Ill, site.	MC	1914	1402	
Morris Gift Shop, San Francisco, Calif.	W	1948	4824	
Mossberg, Herman T, South Bend, Ind.	E	1949	4914	
Muirhead, Robert, Plato Center, Ill.	MC	1950	5019	
Municipal Boathouse, Madison, Wisc, site.	UGL	1893	9308	58
Munkwitz Duplex, Milwaukee, Wisc, site.	UGL	1916	1606	79
Nakoma Country Club, Madison, Wisc, site.	UGL	1924	2403	52
Neils, Henry J, Minneapolis, Minn.	UGL	1950	5020	22
Nichols, Frederick D, Flossmoor, Ill.	MC	1906	0607	
Northome, Little House, site.	UGL	1913	1304	137
Little House, Library, Allentown, Penn.	E/UGL	1978	1304	137
Little House, Living Room, New York City, NY.	E/UGL	1982	1304	137
Oboler, Gatehouse, Malibu, Calif.	W	1941	4112	

Ocatillo Camp, Chandler, Ariz, site.	W	1928	2702	
Odawara Hotel, Japan, site.	W	1917	1706	
Olfelt, Paul, St Louis Park, Minn.	UGL	1958	5820	21
Palmer, William, Ann Arbor, Mich.	UGL	1950	5021	118
Pappas, Theodore A, St Louis, Mo.	W	1955	5516	
Park Ridge Country Club, Park Ridge, Ill, site.	MC	1912	1204	
Parker, Robert P, Oak Park, Ill.	MC	1892	9206	
Parkwyn Village, Kalamazoo, Mich.	UGL	1948	4806	124
Pauson, Rose, Phoenix, Ariz, site.	W	1940	4011	
Pearce, Wilbur, Bradbury, Calif.	W	1951	5114	
Pebbles and Balch shop, Oak Park, Ill, site.	MC	1907	0708	
Penfield, Louis, Willoughby Hills, Ohio.	E	1953	5303	
Perry, Charles R, Glencoe, Ill.	MC	1915	1516	
Peterson, Seth, Lake Delton, Wisc.	UGL	1958	5821	37
Pettit Memorial Chapel, Belvidere, Ill.	UGL	1906	0619	136
Pettit Memorial Chapel, Belvidere, Ill.	MC	1906	0619	
Pew, John C, Shorewood Hills, Wisc.	UGL	1940	4012	64
Pieper, Arthur, Paradise Valley, Phoenix, Ariz.	W	1952	5218	
Pilgrim Congregational Church, Redding, Calif.	W	1959	5318	
Pitkin, EH, Desbarats, Ontario, Canada.	UGL	1900	0005	96
Plaza Hotel Apartment, FLW, New York City, NY.	E	1954	5532	
Pope-Leighy, Woodlawn, Virginia.	E	1940	4013	
Porter, Andrew T, Spring Green, Wisc.	UGL	1907	0709	48
Post Office, Marin County, Calif.	W	1957	5746	
Post, Fredreick B, Barrington Hills, Ill.	MC	1957	5518	
Pratt, Eric, Galesburg, Mich.	UGL	1948	4827	120
Price, Harold Jr, Bartlesville, Okla.	W	1954	5421	
Price, Harold, Sr, Paradise Valley, Phoenix, Ariz.	W	1954	5421	
Price Tower, Bartelsville, Okla.	W	1952	5215	
Ras El Bar, Egypt, site.	E	1927	7211	
Ravine Bluffs Development, Glencoe, Ill.	MC	1915	1516	
Rayward, John L, New Canaan, Conn.	E	1955	5523	
Rebhuhn, Ben, Great Neck Estates, NY.	E	1937	3801	
Reisley, Roland, Pleasantville, NY.	E	1951	5115	
Richards, Duplex Apartments, Milwaukee, Wisc.	UGL	1916	1605	80
Richards, Small House, Milwaukee, Wisc.	UGL	1916	1605	81

Richards, Bungalow, Burleigh, Wilmette, Ill.	MC	1916	1506	
Milwaukee, Wisc.	UGL	1916	1605	82
Hunt, Stephen MB, Oshkosh, Wisc.	UGL	1917	1703	35
Lake Bluff, Ill.	MC	1916	1506	
Richards, Two-Story House, Smith, Chicago, Ill.	MC	1916	1506	
Hyde, Chicago, Ill.	MC	1916	1506	
Johnson, Evanston, Ill.	MC	1916	1506	
Wyant, Gary, Ind.	MC	1916	1506	
Meier, Monona, Iowa.	W	1916	1506	
Richardson, Stuart, Glen Ridge, NJ.	E	1941	4104	
River Forest Golf Club, Ill, site.	MC	1898	9802	
River Forest Tennis Club, Ill.	MC	1906	0510	
Riverview Terrace Restaurant, Spring Green, Wisc.	UGL	1956	5619	45
Roberts, Abby Beecher, Marquette, Mich.	UGL	1936	3603	97
Roberts, Charles E, Oak Park, Ill.	MC	1896	9603	
Roberts, Isabel, River Forest, Ill.	MC	1908	0808	
Robie, Frederick C, Chicago, Ill.	MC	1909	0908	
Rockyroost, Lamp, Robert M, Madison, site.	UGL	1893	9301	58

The American Systems Buildings, 1916

Roloson, Robert W, Rowhouses, Chicago, Ill.	MC	1894	9404	
Romeo and Juliet Windmill, Spring Green, Wisc.	UGL	1896	9607	49
Rookery Building, Chicago, Ill.	MC	1905	0511	
Root, Hollis R, Glencoe, Ill.	MC	1916	1605	
Rosenbaum, Florence, Ala.	E	1939	3903	
Ross, Charles S, Delavan, Wisc.	UGL	1902	0206	70
Ross, William F, Glencoe, Ill.	MC	1915	1516	
Roux Library, Florida Southern College, Lakeland, Fla.	E	1941	3805	
Rubin, Nathan, Canton, Ohio.	E	1951	5116	
Rudin, Walter, Madison, Wisc.	UGL	1957	5706	61
St Marks in the Bowrie, New York City, NY, site.	E	1929	2905	
San Marcos in the Desert, site.	W	1928	2704	
Sander, Frank S, Stamford, Conn.	E	1953	5304	
Schaberg, Donald, Okemos, Mich.	UGL	1950	5022	111
Schultz, Carl, St Joseph, Mich.	UGL	1957	5745	130
Schwartz, Bernard, Two Rivers, Wisc.	UGL	1939	3904	36
Scoville Park Fountain, Oak Park, Ill.	MC	1903	0305	
Scully, Vincent, site.	E	1948	4816	
Serlin, Edward, Pleasantville, NY.	E	1949	4917	
Shavin, Seamour, Chattanooga, Tenn.	E	1950	5023	
Smith Bank, Dwight, Ill.	E	1905	0512	
Smith, George W, Oak Park, Ill.	MC	1896	9803	
Smith, Melvin Maxwell, Bloomfield Hills, Mich.	UGL	1949	4818	116
Smith, Richard, Jefferson, Wisc.	UGL	1959	5026	65
Snowflake, Wall, Carlton D, Plymouth, Mich.	UGL	1941	4114	113
Sondern, Clarence, Kansas City, Mo.	W	1940	4014	
Spencer, Dudley, Wilmington, Delaware.	E	1956	5605	
Spencer, George W, Delavan, Wisc.	UGL	1902	0207	69
Staley, Karl A, North Madison, Ohio.	E	1951	5119	
Steffens, Oscar, Chicago, site.	MC	1909	0909	
Steinway Hall, Chicago, Ill, site.	MC			
Stevens, C Leigh, Auldbrass Plantation, Yemassee, SC.	E	1940	4015	
Stewart, George C, Monteceto, Calif.	W	1909	0907	
Stockman, GC, Mason City, Iowa.	W	1908	0809	

Stohr Arcade, Chicago, site.	MC	1909	0910	
Storer, John, Los Angeles, Hollywood, Calif.	W	1923	2304	
Stromquist, Donald, Bountiful, Utah.	W	1958	5626	
Sturges, Brentwood Heights, Calif.	W	1939	3905	
Sullivan, Louis, Albert, Chicago, Ill.	MC	1892	9207	
Sullivan, Louis, Ocean Springs, Miss.	E	1890	9003	
Sugarloaf Mountain, Strong, Maryland, site.	E	1924	2505	
Sunday, Robert H, Marshalltown, Iowa.	W	1955	5522	
Suntop Homes, Ardmore, Penn.	E	1939	3906	
Sutton, Harvey P, McCook, Nebr.	W	1907	0710	
Sweeton, JA, Cherry Hill, NJ.	E	1959	5027	
Taliesin, Spring Green, Wisc.	UGL	1911	1104	42
Taliesin West, Scottsdale, Ariz.	W	1938	3803	
Tan-y-deri, Porter, Andrew D, Spring Green, Wisc.	UGL	1907	0709	48
Teater, Archie B, Bliss, Idaho.	W	1952	5211	
Thaxton, William L, Bunker Hill, Texas.	W	1954	5414	
Thomas, Frank W, Oak Park, Ill.	MC	1901	0106	
Thurber Art Gallery, Chicago, Ill, site.	MC	1909	0911	

Courtyard, Taliesin, Spring Green, Wisc, c1918

Tirranna, Rayward, John, New Canaan, Conn.	E	1955	5523	
Tomek, Ferdinand F, Riverside, Ill.	MC	1907	0711	
Tonkens, Gerald B, Amberly Village, Ohio.	E	1955	5510	
Tracy, William B, Normandy Park, Wash.	W	1955	5512	
Trier, Paul J, Johnston, Des Moines, Iowa.	W	1957	5724	
Turkel, H, Detroit, Mich.	UGL	1955	5513	117
Unitarian Meeting House, Shorewood Hills, Wisc.	UGL	1947	5031	62
Unity Chapel, Spring Green, Wisc.	UGL	1886	8601	50
Unity Temple, Oak Park, Ill.	MC	1906	0611	
Usonian Exhibition House, New York, NY.	E	1953	5314	
Usonia Homes, Pleasantville, NY.	E	1947	4720	
Van Tamlen, Eugene, Madison, Wisc.	UGL	1956	5518	60
Vosburgh, Ernest, Grand Beach, Mich.	UGL	1916	1607	132
Walker, Clinton, Carmel, Calif.	W	1951	5122	
Wall, Carlton D, Plymouth, Mich.	UGL	1941	4114	113
Waller Apartments, Chicago, Ill.	MC	1895	9504	
Waller Bathing Pavilion, Charlevoix, Mich, site.	UGL	1909	0916	100
Waller, Edward C, River Forest, Ill, site.	MC	1899	9902	

Courtyard, Taliesin, Spring Green, Wisc, c*1980*

Wallis, Henry, Delavan, Wisc.	UGL	1900	0114	73
Walser, JJ, Chicago, Ill.	MC	1903	0306	
Walter, Lowel, Quasqueton, Iowa.	W	1945	4505	
Walton, Robert G, Modesto, Calif.	W	1957	5623	
Weisblatt, David I, Galesburg, Mich.	UGL	1948	4918	123
Weltzheimer, Charles T, Oberlin, Ohio.	E	1948	4819	
Western Pennsylvania Conservancy, Fallingwater.	E	1936	3602	
Westhope, Jones, Richard Lloyd, Tulsa, Okla.	W	1929	2902	
Westcott, Burton J, Springfield, Ohio.	E	1907	0712	
Wiley, Malcom E, Minneapolis, Minn.	UGL	1933	3401	23
Williams, Chauncey, River Forest, Ill.	MC	1895	9505	
Willits, Ward W, Highland Park, Ill.	MC	1901	0208	
Wilson, Abraham, Millstone, NJ.	E	1954	5402	
Winn, Robert D, Kalamazoo, Mich.	UGL	1948	4815	126
Winslow, Herman, River Forest, Ill.	MC	1894	9305	
Women's Building, Spring Green, Wisc, site.	UGL	1914	1413	40
Wooley, Francis, Oak Park, Ill.	MC	1893	9405	
World's Columbian Exhibition of 1893, Chicago, Ill.	MC			
Wright, David, Phoenix, Ariz.	E	1950	5030	
Wright, Duey, Wausau, Wisc.	UGL	1957	5727	33
Wright, Frank Lloyd,				
Studio, Los Angeles, Calif, site.	W	1922	2201	
House and Studio, Oak Park, Ill.	MC	1889	8901	
Studio, Chicago, Ill, site.	MC	1911	1113	
Apartment, Plaza, NY, site.	E	1954	5532	
Wright Robert Llewellyn, Bethesda, Maryland	E	1953	5312	
Wyoming Valley Grammar School,				
Spring Green, Wisc.	UGL	1957	5741	51
Wynants, Wilber, Gary, Ind.	MC	1915	1506	
Yahara Boat Club, Madison, Wisc, site.	UGL	1905	0211	58
Yamamura, Tazaemon, Ashiya, Osaka, Japan.	W	1918	1803	
Young, Harrison P, Oak Park, Ill.	MC	1895	9507	
Zeigler, Jessie R, Frankfort, Kent.	E	1910	1007	
Zimmerman, Isadore, Manchester, NH.	E	1952	5214	

Minnesota Cities

Austin, near Rochester
    SP Elam House   30
Cloquet, near Duluth
    RW Lindholm House   19
    Lindholm Service Station   18
Deephaven, near Minneapolis
    Francis W Little House original site   137
Hastings, near Minneapolis
    Fasbender Medical Clinic   26
Minneapolis; see also St Louis Park, Stillwater
    Henry J Neils House   22
    Malcom E Wiley House   23
Rochester
    AH Bubilian House   29
    James B McBean House   27
    Thomas E Keys House   28
Stillwater, near Minneapolis
    Donald Lovness Cottage   25
    Donald Lovness House   24
St Joseph, near St Cloud
    Dr Edward LaFond House   20
St Louis Park, near Minneapolis
    Paul Olfelt House   21

Wisconsin Cities

Bayside, north of Milwaukee
    Joseph Mollica House   77
Beaver Dam, northeast of Madison
    Arnold Jackson House new site   67
Columbus, northeast of Madison
    E Clarke Arnold House   66
Delavan, north of Lake Geneva
    AP Johnson House   74
    Fred B Jones Gatehouse   71
    Fred B Jones House   72
    Lake Delavan Yacht Club site   68
    Charles S Ross House   70
    George W Spencer House   69
    Henry Wallis Cottage   73
Dousman, west of Milwaukee
    Maurice Greenberg House   75
Fox Point, north of Milwaukee